Rethinking Children, Violence and Safeguarding

Lorraine Radford

New Childhoods Series

ANDOVER COLLEGE

continuum

Continuum International Publishing Group

The Tower Building   80 Maiden Lane
11 York Road   Suite 704
London SE1 7NX   New York NY 10038

www.continuumbooks.com

British Library Cataloguing-in-Publication Data
A catalogue record for this book is available from the British Library.

ISBN: 978-1-4411-6890-0 (hardcover)
        978-1-8470-6558-2 (paperback)

Library of Congress Cataloging-in-Publication Data
A catalog record for this book is available from the Library of Congress.

Typeset by Fakenham Prepress Solutions, Fakenham, Norfolk NR21 8NN
Printed and bound in India

Contents

Introduction to New Childhoods series

The amount of current attention given to children and to childhood is unprecedented. Recent years have seen the agreement of new international conventions, national bodies established, and waves of regional and local initiatives all concerning children.

This rapid pace has been set by many things. Demand from children themselves, from adults working with children, from governments and global bodies, new ideas and raw needs: all are fuelling change. Within and, often, leading the movement is research. From the work of multinational corporations designed to reach into the minds of children and the pockets of parents, through to charity-driven initiatives aiming to challenge the forces that situate children in extreme poverty, a massive amount of energy is expended in research relating to children and their lives. Research can be seen as original investigation undertaken in order to gain knowledge and understanding through a systematic and rigorous process of critical enquiry examining 'even the most commonplace assumption' (Kellett, 2005, p. 9). This attention is not all benign. As Kellett has pointed out, the findings can be used by the media to saturate and accost, rather than support under-12s who are seen as 'obese', for example, or to stigmatize young people by the use of statistics. However, research can also play a role in investigating, enquiring, communicating and understanding for the benefit of children and young people. Recent years have seen innovations in the focus of research, as political moves that challenge the ways in which children have been silenced and excluded result in previously unseen pictures of children's experiences of poverty, family life or community. The attitudes, opinions and lived experiences of children are being given air, and one of the themes within the 'New Childhoods' series concerns the opportunities and challenges this is creating. As this book will reveal, research is being used to set new agendas, to challenge ways of living and working that oppress, harm or limit children. It is also being used to test preconceptions and long-held beliefs about children's lived experiences. In addition to the focus of research, innovations are being made in the way research is conceived and carried out. Its role in children's lives is changing. In the past much research treated children as objects; research was done on them, with the agenda and framework set purely by adults. New work is emerging where children create the way in which research is conceived and carried out. Children act as researchers, and researchers work with questions formulated by children or work with children.

This series aims to offer access to some of the challenges, discoveries and work-in-progress of contemporary research. The terms *child* and *childhood* are used within the series in line with Article 1 of the United Nations Convention on the Rights of the Child which defines 'children' as persons up to the age of 18. The books offer opportunities to engage with emerging ideas, questions and practices. They will help those studying childhood, or living and working with children to become familiar with challenging work, to engage with findings and to reflect on their own ideas, experiences and ways of working.

Phil Jones, Institute of Education, University of London, UK

Preface

This book is about children and violence, covering the victimization of children as well as children who use violence towards others. It aims to address a need within the area of 'new childhood studies' where to date little has been written specifically about the social construction of violence and 'childhood'. The aim of the book is to give readers a critical overview of key developments in research, policy and practice on children and violence in the context of the recent major shifts in thinking from child protection towards early intervention, safeguarding and prevention, and evidencing better outcomes. How we 'think' about children and disembodied, fragmented and de-gendered thinking about violence has had a profound impact on actions against the abuse of children and our treatment of children who commit violence.

The book brings together theory, policy, research and practice issues from a range of subject areas relevant to understanding violence in childhood. I hope the book will be of interest to general readers as well as those studying for qualifications in social science, social work, childhood studies, psychology, health and criminology.

The book has been designed to encourage reflective learning. Summary points, critical questions and examples of theory and research are included at various points in the text for readers who would like to review and reflect on the issues covered. Each chapter provides some recommended further readings for those who want to extend their learning.

Part 1 identifies the key debates and the questions that will be considered throughout the book. Key definitions and the historical context in which concerns about violence and childhood developed are briefly considered in Chapter 1.

Part 2 provides an interdisciplinary review of research and scholarship. The major focus of the book will be on children and violence in the UK; however, international research literature and policy developments are included where relevant and where this adds to our understanding. Chapter 2 reviews research and scholarly works that consider the question 'Why are some children violent?' Chapter 3 reviews research and scholarly works on the causes of violence and maltreatment of children.

In Part 3 the implications for children's lives are considered. Chapter 4 reviews research on the impact and consequences for children's well-being of living with violence and maltreatment. Chapter 5 explores public attitudes on violence towards and by children and the positioning of children as 'victims' or 'villains'. Chapter 6 looks at the framing of childhood violence in recent UK crime prevention policies in public and in cyberspace, and the consequences of these policies for children's lives. Chapter 7 explores the expansion and differentiation in the focus of child protection and the shift towards early intervention, safeguarding and prevention, and looks at how policies on keeping safe have affected children's lives.

Throughout the book, materials from research are used to illustrate how children's voices and participation can challenge us all to rethink our approaches to their experiences of violence.

Part 1
Debates, Dilemmas and Challenges: the Background to Children and Violence

Chapter Outline

Introduction and key questions

Violence by and towards children has been given a lot of media attention in recent years, and the following Box contains newspaper and website extracts as examples of this.

Childhood under siege?

'Unstable' mother let baby starve to death An inquest has heard how an 11-month-old baby was found starved to death in his cot after social workers left him in the care of his mentally unstable mother. The boy's emaciated body was discovered by paramedics at a council flat strewn with rubbish and dirty nappies in St John's Wood on March 8 last year. The child was on Westminster council's at-risk register and his 29-year-old mother had been assessed by doctors, social workers, mental health workers and health visitors in the months before his death.

Evening Standard London, 9 March 2011

⇨

Childhood under siege?—Cont'd

Teenager 'hunted to death by gang' 15-year-old Zac Olumegbon was hunted down and stabbed to death near his school in South Norwood, south London by four members of a rival gang, the Old Bailey has heard. The boy was stabbed four times through the heart and neck and died in a garden of a house on July 2 last year. Four youths, two aged 17, one 16 and one 15, deny murder. The trial continues.

Metro London, 10 March 2011

The creation of a probationary license for adults through the national vetting scheme exacerbates the breakdown of trust within communities and throws assumptions about adult authority and responsibility into question in a way that mitigates against people stepping in to help children when things go wrong.

Furedi and Bristow, 2008, p. 55

The above extracts illustrate two divergent views about the impact of violence in children's lives. The first is a view of prevalent violence towards and by children which is largely seen to have its root cause in poor parenting/inadequate mothering. Here the plights of children in the first extract and of baby Peter Connelly tortured and brutally killed by their supposed 'caregivers', are ignored by both the community and professionals.[1] Poorly parented, out of control and fearful youth alike, repeating a downward spiral of intergenerational violence and neglect, need to carry knives to survive in an utterly hostile environment. The alternative view, illustrated in the extract from Furedi and Bristow, suggests that the risks of violence are disproportionate, create unnecessary fear, disempower parents and destroy relationships between adults and children. From this perspective, vetting and barring procedures to protect children from abusers and sex offenders who get into positions of trust in order to get access to their victims, parental fears about 'stranger-danger' and institutional risk aversion work together to confine children, prevent them from doing anything remotely adventurous, and limit their opportunities and interactions with adults in their communities. The risk-averse society is supposed to have caused a climate of terror among adults about being suspected of paedophilia and created a tangle of red tape that deters anyone wanting to volunteer to work with or look after anyone else's children. Both approaches suggest that childhood is under siege, from either the 'reality' of violence in a polarized globalized world or from our efforts to control it through risk-management activities. What sense are those working with children to make of these divergent positions?

Key questions considered in this chapter will be:

- What is 'violence'?
- What is helpful to know about the risks of violence when working or interacting with children and young people?
- What is the prevalence of violence and abuse in the UK today?
- Is the world a more dangerous place where children experience more violence and commit more violent crime than ever before?
- Are the risks of violence to and violence by children exaggerated and does this limit children's freedom?

What is violence?

The focus of this book is on working with children and young people who are affected by crime, violence and abuse. Defining crime is technically more straightforward than defining what is an act of violence or abuse. Crime is simply any act, or failure to act, that is criminal. It involves a breach of rules defined by the state or by law and is usually subject to sanction, conviction or punishment. We will return in later chapters to consider the specific issues for children in determining responsibility for and dealing with criminal behaviour.

Defining violence is not straightforward because what is or is not considered as being violent changes over time, across cultures, according to context and according to whose voices matter in defining what is legitimate, normalized or abuse. While it may be possible to get a general consensus that certain extreme acts of behaviour such as killing another person are indeed acts of violence there is a whole range of behaviour besides where opinions will be more divided.

Activity

Read the scenarios below and consider:
What is/is not violence or abuse?
What is/is not a crime?

- A parent or an adult smacking an 8-year-old-boy.
- A 5-year-old girl hitting her 8-year-old sister or hitting an 8-year-old-boy at school.

⇨

Activity—Cont'd

- A 16-year-old boy loses his family and becomes a refugee during armed conflict in Iraq
- A girl having sex with her boyfriend but feeling pushed into it by things he said or did
- A mother frightening her child by telling her the bogeyman will get her if she is not good
- Class mates calling a girl names and making fun of her on Facebook
- A 15-year-old-boy physically restrained by adults working in the secure accommodation where he currently lives
- A woman throwing a plate at her husband during an argument about money
- A man sending his estranged partner a bunch of flowers
- A 17-year-old-girl commits suicide in a detention centre
- A 14-year-old-boy going to school in dirty clothes every day because he has been sleeping on friends' sofas since his mother's new boyfriend moved in.

Does the context and the relationship in which the behaviour takes place influence your view on what is or is not violent? What if you change the ages of the young people in each scenario so that they are younger, teenagers or adults?

A question that may initially be raised from these scenarios is whether our focus is on interpersonal acts of violence or whether we should consider institutional and state-initiated acts of violence such as warfare, armed conflict and the treatment of young people in custody within penal institutions.

The World Health Organization has defined violence as being:

> the intentional use of physical force or power, threatened or actual, against oneself, another person, or against a group or community, that either results in or has a high likelihood of resulting in injury, death, psychological harm, maldevelopment, or deprivation.
>
> (Krug *et al.*, 2002)

The WHO identifies a typology of violence with four modes in which violence may be inflicted: physical; sexual; psychological attack; and deprivation, and three subcategories defined by the victim–perpetrator relationship—self-directed violence (self-harm and suicide), interpersonal violence (where one individual harms another in the family, a relationship or community) and collective violence (where individuals or groups commit social, economic or political violence including warfare, civil conflict and discriminations).

Reflections

Activity 1

In what circumstances would you consider this to be an act of violence or abuse? Make a list of the factors that you see as being relevant.

Activity 2

We will illustrate the relevance of context by considering the physical punishment of children by parents or in schools cross-culturally.

- In countries such as Norway, there exists a statutory ban on physical punishment of children by parents and in schools.
- In England, teachers do not have legal powers to physically punish pupils but parents are permitted to use reasonable punishment to discipline a child.
- In Egypt and China, physical punishment of children in schools is against the law but is widely practised.
- In many states in the USA, parents and teachers are not prevented by law from using corporal punishment towards children.

What might be the arguments for and against the approaches taken to the physical punishment of children by adults in each of these countries?

Are the same arguments applicable to a husband's physical violence towards his wife?

The motivation or intent behind an act, particularly intent to cause harm, is clearly highly relevant to what is classified as being criminal and abusive behaviour, although ultimately the state has power to define, and legitimize, acts of violence and abuse. Violence exists on a continuum and its impact will vary with the severity, extent of physical force, frequency of the behaviour and the potential for harm where there are power imbalances between the perpetrator(s) and the victim. Violence may be a single act or omission which has potential to cause harm, or it can be a pattern of behaviour. Thus, for instance, a man sending his estranged partner flowers could be an attempt to reconcile or it could be part of a pattern of harassment that has very harmful psychological consequences if his partner had fled because of the man's domestic violence. The flowers may be a threat rather than a romantic gesture, causing psychological harm by heightening her fear. Talking about the bogeyman is unlikely to frighten an adult partner. Doing this with your child might be harmless game playing, as in the playground game 'What's the Time Mr Wolf?' Talking about the bogeyman could also be part of a pattern of terrorizing mind games and emotional cruelty towards a child. Risks of abuse and violence towards children are intrinsically linked with their dependency relationship with parents, caregivers and adults.

The definition of violence has objective and subjective elements because the harm caused to the victim by another person's act or omissions has to be considered. The relationship between the abuser and the victim will have an influence on the impact and the potential for harm. In a close family or intimate relationship, there is increased scope for the instigator to cause damage and psychological harm. However, traditionally acts of violence and abuse within the family and in close interpersonal relationships have been treated differently and many, until recently, were 'no crimed' (Edwards, 1989). It is still very rare for acts of parental or caregiver abuse to a child to be criminally prosecuted, cases tend to dealt with outside the criminal justice system as child welfare or child protection matters (Finkelhor, 2008).

There are aspects of behaviour which may be considered as 'violence ' or 'abuse' that are particularly harmful to children and young people because children have this developmental dependency on adults. Neglect is a form of deprivation abuse experienced by vulnerable adults, and for children it is the most commonly recorded reason for involvement with child protection services (DCSF, 2010). Child neglect is defined in *Working Together to Safeguard Children*, the government guidance for professionals on child protection, as failing to provide for a child's health, education, emotional development, nutrition, clothing, shelter, safety and safe living conditions, including exclusion of the child from the home and abandonment (DCSF, 2010). Motivation is relevant in determining violence and abuse but it may not be as relevant in cases of neglect where the harmful consequences for the child are part of a creeping condition of lack of care and attention caused by ignorance or ineptitude and not always by malevolence.

Another example of a form of abuse experienced very differently by children and young people is emotional abuse. This covers a wide range of treatment likely to harm the child emotionally including bullying, frightening, corrupting or making fun of a child and treating them with hostility, coldness or contempt. Under the Adoption and Children Act 2002 s120, a child's exposure to domestic violence, namely seeing or overhearing abuse of another person, is recognized as having potential to cause significant harm to a child's well-being.

What is considered to be 'violent' has a normative or 'socially acceptable' element. Violence towards children that was in earlier times deemed to be 'acceptable' in the UK, such as using corporal punishment in education settings, is now condemned. Children are less likely to be openly beaten by adults 'for their own good' than they were in the past. Children and young people in the UK however still lack the right enjoyed by adults to equal protection from violence because the state condones parental use of physical violence towards children as 'reasonable punishment'. Different societies have varied views about violence that can be tolerated towards children. In many countries of the world, parents, and other adults such as teachers, penal staff or care staff are still able to use physical violence to chastise children and young people. Twenty-nine countries, however, have passed legislation banning 'smacking' or parental corporal punishment of children.

Physical punishment of children

Physical punishment of children occurs in the home, in schools, in the penal system and in alternative care.

Table 1.1 Progress on the prohibition of all corporal punishment of children (December 2010)

StaStatus	Prohibited in home	Prohibited in school	Prohibited as penal sentence	Prohibited as discipline in penal system	Prohibited in alternative care
Prohibited	29	110	152	109	38
Not prohibited	168	87	42	78	156
Legality unknown	–	–	3	10	3

Full prohibition of the physical punishment of children, including parental punishment, has been achieved in Austria, Bulgaria, Costa Rica, Croatia, Cyprus, Denmark, Finland, Germany, Greece, Hungary, Iceland, Israel, Kenya, Latvia, Liechtenstein, Luxembourg, Netherlands, New Zealand, Norway, Poland, Portugal, Republic of Muldova, Romania, Spain, Sweden, Tunisia, Ukraine, Uruguay and Venezuala.

Ireland is committed to full prohibition, although the timescale has not been given. In Scotland, the criminal Justice Scotland Act 2003 restricts parents' use of the common law defence with the concept of 'justifiable assault' of a child, defining blows to the head, shaking and use of implements as unjustifiable.

⇨

Physical punishment of children—Cont'd

In England and Wales, the Children Act 2004 maintains reasonable punishment as a defence against charges of common assault.

In Northern Ireland similar provisions are made by the Law Reform (Miscellaneous Provisions) (Northern Ireland) Order 2006.

Source: Global Initiative to End all Corporal Punishment of Children (2010)

What is helpful to know about the risks of violence when working or interacting with children and young people?

Developmental issues affect children's and young people's experiences of victimization as well as their behaviour towards others. Child protection services have focused on parent and caregiver abuse because young children are more vulnerable to abuse from a caregiver who will have greater access to the child, and the opportunity to cause harm and evade detection than other perpetrators. As children grow and their contact with other people outside the home increases, they are exposed to a wider range of potential perpetrators, such as neighbours, teachers, strangers and associates. Children and young people experience and also instigate a lot of interpersonal violence which also varies developmentally. Very young children use aggression instrumentally because they lack the cognitive ability and social skills to negotiate and understand the impact of violence upon others. Children under the age of 8 use physical violence to resolve conflict over possessions while adolescents and teenagers may use it for strategically different purposes in territorial disputes or in relationships (Kiselica and Morill-Richards, 2007). While some forms of physical violence by children and young people, such as sibling violence, commonly decrease in prevalence after the age of 9 or 10, peer violence, especially physical and sexual violence, increases in prevalence during teens (Finkelhor *et al.*, 2009; Radford *et al.*, 2011).

Since at least the nineteenth century, juvenile offending and parenting policies have been influenced by the understanding that children and young people, with appropriate adult guidance, will 'grow out of' violence and other forms of deviant behaviour (Donzelot, 1980; Muncie, 1998). The early identification of problematic violence or harmful behaviour in children and young people, and distinguishing between 'normal' and 'abnormal' behaviour has become a rapidly expanding area of interest for social policy and developmental research (see e.g. Moffitt *et al.*, 2002) and this is a subject to which we will later return. It is a reason for treating young offenders differently.

Abuse and violence perpetrated by other young people is not necessarily less harmful than that perpetrated by adults. Common acts of childhood physical violence, such as sibling violence, are often assumed not to be harmful and part of a young person's developmental process, the process of learning to deal with personal conflicts and disputes (Kiselica and Morill-Richards, 2007). Research suggests that most sibling violence is indeed perceived by young people to be relatively minor; however, this is not case for all sibling violence and certainly not for a lot of peer abuse (Finkelhor *et al.*, 2006). School-based peer abuse or 'bullying' is one of the most common reasons prompting children to call ChildLine (ChildLine, 2011) and, as media reports on suicides of bullied young people have shown, it can have devastating consequences for the mental health and well-being of young people. The adverse consequences for mental health can be identified in very young children (Arsenault *et al.*, 2006).

The impact of violence upon an individual will vary in relation to the severity of an attack and the size or power differentials that may exist between the instigator and the victim. While it may be relatively straightforward to measure the injuries resulting from a physical attack, the impact of violence is very often also psychological. Immediate reactions include fear, anger or upset. Mental health or behavioural consequences can affect a person's opportunities and well-being over the longer term. The consequences for an individual will vary in relation to a number of factors that may compound or help alleviate the impact, including their vulnerabilities, personal resources, access to help and social support. Research on child abuse and neglect has shown that children and young people even in the same family are affected differently and some young people have resilience that helps to mitigate the adverse consequences (Bentovim *et al.*, 2009; Haggerty *et al.*, 1996). This issue of resilience will be discussed further in later chapters of this book.

The box below provides some basic definitions of violence and maltreatment relevant to working with children and young people.

Definitions of violence and maltreatment

Child maltreatment as defined by the WHO

All forms of physical and/or emotional ill treatment, sexual abuse, neglect or negligent treatment or commercial or other exploitation, resulting in actual

⇨

Definitions of violence and maltreatment—Cont'd

or potential harm to the child's health, survival, development or dignity in the context of a relationship of responsibility, trust or power.

(Butchart *et al.*, 2006, p. 59)

Working Together definition of physical abuse to a child

Physical abuse may involve hitting, shaking, throwing, poisoning, burning or scalding, drowning, suffocating, or otherwise causing physical harm to a child. Physical harm may also be caused when a parent or carer fabricates the symptoms of, or deliberately induces, illness in a child.

(DCSF, 2010, p. 38)

Working Together definition of child sexual abuse

[Child sexual abuse] Involves forcing or enticing a child or young person to take part in sexual activities, not necessarily involving a high level of violence, whether or not the child is aware of what is happening. The activities may involve physical contact, including assault by penetration (for example, rape or oral sex) or non-penetrative acts such as masturbation, kissing, rubbing and touching outside of clothing. They may also include non-contact activities, such as involving children in looking at, or in the production of, sexual images, watching sexual activities, encouraging children to behave in sexually inappropriate ways, or grooming a child in preparation for abuse (including via the internet).

(DCSF, 2010, p. 38)

Working Together definition of emotional abuse

Emotional abuse is the persistent emotional maltreatment of a child such as to cause severe and persistent adverse effects on the child's emotional development. It may involve conveying to children that they are worthless or unloved, inadequate, or valued only insofar as they meet the needs of another person. It may include not giving the child opportunities to express their views, deliberately silencing them or 'making fun' of what they say or how they communicate. It may feature age or developmentally inappropriate expectations being imposed on children. These may include interactions that are beyond the child's developmental capability, as well as overprotection and limitation of exploration and learning, or preventing the child participating in normal social interaction. It may involve seeing or hearing the ill-treatment of another. It may involve serious bullying (including cyberbullying), causing children frequently to feel frightened or in danger, or the exploitation or corruption of children. Some level of emotional abuse is involved in all types of maltreatment of a child, though it may occur alone.

(DCSF, 2010, p. 38)

⇨

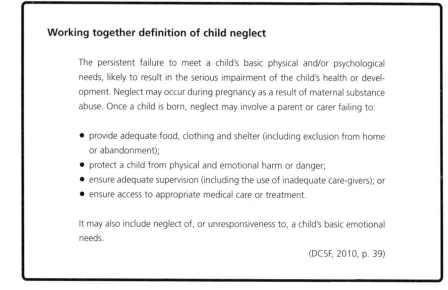

Working together definition of child neglect

The persistent failure to meet a child's basic physical and/or psychological needs, likely to result in the serious impairment of the child's health or development. Neglect may occur during pregnancy as a result of maternal substance abuse. Once a child is born, neglect may involve a parent or carer failing to:

- provide adequate food, clothing and shelter (including exclusion from home or abandonment);
- protect a child from physical and emotional harm or danger;
- ensure adequate supervision (including the use of inadequate care-givers); or
- ensure access to appropriate medical care or treatment.

It may also include neglect of, or unresponsiveness to, a child's basic emotional needs.

(DCSF, 2010, p. 39)

There are no absolute criteria for determining what might be harmful to the health, development or well-being of a child or young person. The concept of significant harm as introduced by the Children Act 1989 provides the threshold for compulsory intervention into family life in the best interests of the child. The consideration of significant harm depends on a number of factors such as the extent of the physical harm, the duration and frequency of the abuse or neglect, the extent of premeditation, the degree of threat, coercion, sadism, etc.

The prevalence of violence in children's lives

Official records of homicides and violent crime indicate an increase in the numbers and the rates per head of population of homicides and crimes of violence against an individual today compared with records from the nineteenth century. The number of homicides in England and Wales doubled between 1898 (328) and 2007/2008 (753) (Home Office, 2009a). Rates per million in the population were fairly consistent from the 1930s to the post-war period, never rising above 8.6

⇨

homicides per million of the population until 1974 when they increased to 10.7 homicides per million of the population, rising to 13 per million in 1995. Homicide rates then fell but exceptional incidents such as the murder of over 170 women by the GP Harold Shipman, the deaths of Chinese cockle pickers at Morecombe bay, the suffocation of Chinese immigrants in a lorry and the London bombings in 2005, as well as the introduction of new crime recording standards in 2003 have inflated the numbers. The latest rate recorded for 2008/2009 was 12 homicides per million of the population. Babies under 12 months old have the highest rates of homicide per head of population, there being 31 homicides of under-1-year-olds per million of the population in 2007/2008. (Home Office, 2009a, 2010).

Police and court records, 'official statistics' on crime, at best only count crimes that are known or reported and recorded by the police, whereas interpersonal violence, for a variety of reasons, often goes unreported and is therefore not counted. The victim may not be able to tell the police, may fear reprisals or may believe that the police will not take them seriously. Adults and children experiencing abuse in the family, even if they call the police for help because they want the violence to stop, may not see any benefit in having the perpetrator arrested (Hoyle, 1998; Mullender *et al.*, 2003).

Child abuse and neglect is more likely to be counted in child protection registration statistics. These are crude indicators of child maltreatment because they only count cases that are identified and considered to be in need of protection by the state/local authority. The number of children on child protection registers in England increased to a peak in 1995. From 1995 to 2005 they fell, and 26 per cent fewer children were registered (35,000 in 1995 cf 29,500 in 2005, or 32 children per 10,000 of child population in 1995 to 24 children per 10,000 of child population in 2006). The numbers have increased substantially since the tragic death of baby Peter Connelly. On March 31 2010 in England there were 38,440 children (excluding unborn) subject to local authority child protection plans (Department of Education, 2010). Around 0.3 per cent of the under-18 population each year are subject to child protection plans.

Victim and offender self-report surveys are other commonly used methods for finding out about how much crime or violence there is. Self-report victimi-zation research on children and young people has many advantages and many flaws. Samples are small and not representative of the wider population, definitions of abuse and the ages of research participants vary, and validated and standard measures of violence and abuse and its impact are seldom used. A high proportion of the research on child abuse is actually based on adult memories of their experiences in childhood (see Finkelhor, 2008).

The first British Crime Survey in England and Wales was published by the Home Office in 1982. This collects information on victimization and crime experiences directly in their homes from people aged over 16. The first survey promoted the belief that fear of crime was exaggerated and that the 'statistically average person' would be likely to be assaulted and 'injured however slightly, once every hundred years' (Hough and Mayhew, 1983). Feminists and some criminologists criticized the Home Office researchers for failing to adequately consider 'hidden' crimes such as domestic and sexual violence towards adult women (Hanmer and Saunders, 1985; Kinsey *et al.*, 1986). The exclusion of children's experiences was not an issue at the time. Information on domestic violence, sexual assault and stalking behaviour towards adults has since been collected (Mirlees-Black, 1999; Walby and Allen, 2004) and is now routinely included, and recently the BCS was extended to include children. Findings when launched were described as 'experimental'.

Example of research

The British Crime Survey was for the first time extended during 2009 to cover children aged 10 to 15. Noting that the levels of victimization reported by children were alarmingly high and would massively increase the BCS estimates on the prevalence of crime, four approaches to classifying crimes experienced by children are outlined in the report:

- *All in law* include all incidents reported by children that are in law a crime; that is, where the victim perceived intent on the part of the perpetrator to inflict hurt or damage or to steal property. There were 2,153,000 in law incidents, 641,000 of which were violence against the person resulting in injury.
- *Norms-based* apply an explicit set of normative rules to exclude relatively minor incidents. These rules were developed from the findings of qualitative research with children but a panel of adults decides what most people would view as a 'crime' to a child. There were 1,055,000 norms-based incidents, 548,000 of which were violence against the person resulting in injury.
- *All in law outside school* include all incidents reported by children that are in law a crime except those occurring in school. This approach is a rough approximation of the guidance issued jointly by the (then) Department for

⇨

Example of research—Cont'd

Children, Schools and Families, Home Office and Association of Chief Police Officers in July 2007 (Home Office, 2009a) which provides that unless the child or the parent/guardian asks for the police to record these crimes (or if the crime is deemed to be more serious) then the matter remains within the school's internal disciplinary processes. This is likely to result in most low-level incidents being dealt with by school authorities and not recorded as crimes by the police. There were 643,000 in law outside school incidents, 249,000 of which were violence against the person resulting in injury.

- *Victim perceived* include all incidents in law defined as a crime that are also thought by victims themselves to be crimes. This is a wholly subjective measure based on the perceptions of the individual child. There were 404,000 victim perceived incidents, 171,000 of which were violence against the person resulting in injury.

(Adapted from Millard and Flatley, 2010)

The victim perceived estimates are consistently lower than the other three. The 'all in law' estimates are consistently higher. (Adapted from Flatley *et al.*, 2010)

Activity

What are the possible explanations for the differences between the rates of victimization as defined by criminal law and the rates based on victim perceptions?

The BCS four-level definitional problem compares 'objective measures' (based on a legal definition of crime or agreed criteria such as injuries or harm) with 'subjective measures' (based on victim perception of an experience as an act of abuse or a crime).

What are the advantages and disadvantages in using objective or subjective measures to research children's experiences of crime, violence and abuse?

These four measures were subsequently adjusted for the next survey to include a 'preferred estimate' that excluded minor offences by peers or by family members without injury or use of a weapon, and a 'broad estimate' that was the all in law approach described above (Chaplin *et al.*, 2011). The BCS did not ask children and young people about sexual abuse or about experiences of violence in the home. Even with the minor offences from family members and peers excluded, children were found to experience much higher rates of violence than adults, 3.1 per cent of adults reporting experiencing violence in the past year compared with 6.9 per cent of 10- to 15-year-olds on the preferred measure or 12.1 per cent with the broad measure (Chaplin *et al.*, 2011).

Recent research by the NSPCC with children and young people included questions on interpersonal violence and abuse.

Example of research—Child Abuse and Neglect in the UK Today

A household survey was conducted for the NSPCC in 2009. Some 6,196 interviews about childhood experiences of maltreatment and victimization were collected from parents reporting for children aged under 11, from children and young people aged 11 to 17 and from young adults aged 18 to 24. The researchers' findings on the rates of maltreatment and victimization reported for children between the ages of 1 month and 18 years and for young adults reporting childhood experiences are given in Table 1.2.

Table 1.2 Prevalence of child maltreatment and victimization

Type of abuse	Caregiver report child aged under 11 lifetime abuse (%)	Caregiver report child aged under 11 past year abuse (%)	Self-reports young people 11 to 17 years lifetime abuse (%)	Self-reports young people 11 to 17 years past year abuse (%)	Self-reports on abuse in childhood by 18- to 24-year-olds (%)
Severe maltreatment by an adult and forced contact sexual abuse any perpetrator	5.9	–	18.6	–	25.3
Maltreatment by parent/guardian	8.9	2.5	21.9	6	24.5
Maltreatment by an adult not living in the home	2.3	1.2	7.8	3.1	12.8
Sexual abuse	1.2	0.6	16.5	9.4	24.1
Intimate partner abuse	–	–	7.9	5	13.4
Victimization by peers	28	20.2	59.5	35.3	63.2
Exposure to parental domestic violence	12	3.2	17.5	2.5	23.7

Source: Radford *et al.* (2011)

⇨

Example of research—Child Abuse and Neglect in the UK Today—Cont'd

There is a sizeable gap between the numbers of maltreated children brought to the attention of child protection services and the numbers reported to have been maltreated in self-report surveys The NSPCC researchers reported the following findings:

- Of those physically hurt by caregivers in childhood, in 22.9 per cent of cases nobody knew about it.
- Of those who experienced contact sexual abuse by an adult in childhood in 34 per cent of cases nobody knew about it.
- Of those who experienced contact sexual abuse from a peer in childhood, in 82.7 per cent of cases nobody else knew about it.

Comparing responses to 26 survey questions used by the NSPCC to research the prevalence of child maltreatment in 1998/1989 and replicated with the young adult sample in 2009, the researchers found no changes in the prevalence of child neglect but a general decline in reported experiences of harsh emotional and physical treatment, and also in experiences of some types of physical and sexual violence.

Activity

Looking at Table 1.1, which perpetrators of maltreatment and victimization would you say are most frequently reported? Do you think they also pose the greatest risks to children's well-being?

Is there more or less child abuse today?

Is the world a more dangerous place where children experience more violence and commit more violent crime than ever before? Has life become more risky for children than it was for previous generations? Are children and young people themselves more likely to break the law and commit acts of violence?

There are empirical difficulties in finding data and statistics to show trends in crime and violence. What is recognized and recorded as crime or as an act of violence has changed over time. Arguably, acts of violence that result in severe, visible injuries or death should be more easily measured, but even homicide rates are difficult to measure accurately over time because collecting data is a recent preoccupation. The first crime statistics were collected in England in 1805 and data from the police started to be systematically collected in 1857 (Emsley, 2005). From the nineteenth century onward official statistics and newspaper reports on crime started to dominate how we think about crime. Press and broadsheet coverage of violent crimes such as 'garrotting' (a form of violent street robbery) in the 1850s and 1860s and cases such as Jack the Ripper's murders of women in Whitechapel in 1888 fuelled public concerns about widespread violent crimes. Crime and violence affecting children and young people historically were not recorded so getting information to demonstrate trends is difficult. Even homicide data and information on the executions of children are severely limited because the crimes may not have been detected and the ages of those involved were sometimes not known or recorded (Emsley, 2005). Many criminologists are reluctant to express an opinion on whether there is more or less crime and violence now than in the past because what gets counted tells us as much about the politics and recording practices of agencies such as the police as about the 'true' level of crime and violence. This is a problem that continues today. Any understanding of how much crime or violence exists has to be based on knowledge of what 'counted' as being worthy of measurement and how the information was collected.

Violence to and by children and young people has most likely happened throughout history but in the nineteenth century both child abuse and the problem of juvenile or youth crime became prominent as social problems. The idea that children and young people should be dealt with differently to adults emerged at this time along with notions of 'adolescence' as a distinct phase in human development (Cunningham, 2006). In 1838 the first penal institution specifically for juvenile boys opened in Parkhurst (Muncie, 1998). Previously, children and young people above the age of 7 had been subject to the death penalty or transported and punished the same as adults. Under the 'bloody code' in the early nineteenth century there were more than 200 capital offences, many of them property crimes. Death sentences were frequently given to children between the ages of 7 and 13 for offences as minor as stealing ribbon; however, sentences were also regularly commuted. It was not until the Children Act 1908 that the age of 16 was stipulated as being the minimum for the death penalty. Sixteen-year-old Harold Wilkins, in 1932, was the last juvenile to be sentenced to death in England (Emsley, 2006).

The 'discovery' of child cruelty and the belief that juvenile offenders should be treated differently to adults were linked with major social and economic and political changes that occurred in the rapidly industrializing and urbanizing landscape of nineteenth century Britain. (Elmsley, 2006; Muncie, 1998; Parton, 1997). There have been three periods of time when the maltreatment of children in the UK has attracted particularly high levels of interest—from the 1870s to about 1914, from the mid 1960s to the late 1980s and in the present day (Parton, 2007). Periods of public concern about and unravelling concepts of violence towards women and child cruelty have coincided with feminist activity and intense campaigning by children's charities such as the NSPCC. Historically it is argued, there has been a polticization of child abuse (Jenks, 1996; Parton, 1985).

In nineteenth century England there was a great deal of concern among wealthier and middle classes about the squalid living conditions, morality and lawlessness of the poor living in industrialized urban areas. Moral contamination of children and young people was a concern that was very apparent in debates about juvenile offending, and brutal, morally degraded working-class family life, where violence towards women and children was seen to be rife (Gordon, 1989). Prior to the family law reforms in the nineteenth century, women and children lacked legal personality, the rights within the patriarchal family residing with husbands and fathers. Women and children were 'property' of the man and he had the common law right to physically chastise them. 'Wife beating', extreme physical violence to wives in the form of 'aggravated assaults', and 'child cruelty', severe physical violence and neglect, were the first acts of family violence to be recognized in legislation passed to protect adult and child victims from 1857 onward. Frances Power Cobbe, a nineteenth-century women's rights and anti-vivisection campaigner, argued for laws to protect women from wife torture in the 'kicking districts' of England and reform of the working-class family to prevent children from repeating the cycle of abuse, poverty and drunkenness (Cobbe, 1878).

It was the horrific physical violence, starvation and neglect of 9-year-old Mary Ellen in the USA in 1874 that precipitated the development of the world's first organization against child cruelty, the New York Society for the Prevention of Cruelty to Children and subsequently, in England, the development of the NSPCC (NSPCC, 2006). Organizations such as Barnados 'rescued' child vagrants from the streets and NSPCC uniformed inspectors gained statutory powers to remove children from their families, although in most cases inspectors aimed to 'reform' the family as there were too many children to take away (Parton, 1997). Child abuse and violence was more noticeable and may well have been worse as urban poverty was very severe and many working-class children's lives were brief and harsh. Children's charities such as the NSPCC and Barnados produced photographs and documentary evidence showing the squalor and cruelty of some children's lives.

Activity

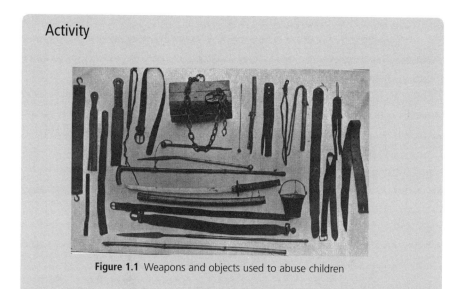

Figure 1.1 Weapons and objects used to abuse children

Consider the range of weapons and objects in Figure 1.1 that were used to abuse children.

- What do the objects tell us about attitudes towards children?
- What do the objects tell us about how child cruelty was understood?

This period saw modernization of the courts and legal system, the development of modern policing and social work, and an increased use of the law (rather than religion) to regulate everyday life and social relationships. There was the development of public health programmes. There were major changes to family life, particularly the promotion, through policy change and educational home visiting by middle-class women, of the 'male breadwinner' model of the family (Lewis, 1996). Women, through a series of employment regulations, trade union activity, education acts and reforms of the family law, became viewed as primarily responsible for childcare, and men for earning a 'family wage' (see Bolt, 1993; Fraser, 1973). Children's lives were separately organized from adults' lives as a series of factory acts and education acts limited and redefined children's spheres of activity and their developmental dependencies on adults within schools and the family. The prison reformer Mary Carpenter helped to promote the belief that reform of juvenile delinquents depended on meeting their needs for care or protection as well as their needs for overt discipline. The oscillation between welfare and justice in the history of policy on juvenile crime and child protection had its roots in this era of rapid change. Welfare approaches stressed helping young people and their families to overcome poverty and disadvantage. The justice approaches focused on control and discipline.

Although legislation was passed to regulate incest in 1908, child sexual abuse by adults and close family members did not really attract a lot of policy interest until well into the twentieth century. Feminists in the late 1970s started to write and talk about sexual abuse (Armstrong, 1978). The identification of a large number of children in Cleveland as potential abuse victims led to wider awareness, controversy and a public enquiry that brought sexual abuse into the core of the child protection business (Campbell, 1988; Smart, 1995).The emotional abuse of children is an even more recent area of child protection activity and research, similarly linked with campaigning by feminists and children's organizations in relation to the impact on children of living with domestic violence. When considering the question of prevalence and how violence affects the lives of children and young people today, we need to bear in mind that the concept of 'violence' experienced by women and children has expanded through history to include a broader range of types of abuse.

Is life more risky for children? What are the issues?

Are the risks of violence to and by children exaggerated and does this limit children's freedom?

One interpretation might be that awareness of violence, of child abuse and of children's offending behaviour has improved so that, taking the long view, life is much less brutal and violent for children today than it was previously. There is empirical evidence that children's health and well-being has improved and child and infant mortality rates are lower today than they were in nineteenth century Britain (Fraser, 1973; Lewis, 1996). Children are treated differently when they come into contact with the criminal justice system. Feminism and children's welfare organizations have uncovered more 'hidden crimes' and we have all learned more about the risks children face. Some argue that increased awareness, public education and child protection activities are the most likely explanation now for an observed decline in some forms of child victimization, especially a decline in child sexual abuse (Finkelhor and Jones, 2006; Finkelhor *et al.*, 2010). It could be argued from this perspective that strategies such as vetting and barring, criticizsed as bureaucratic and disproportionate, have helped to raise awareness about, and possibly regulate, adults in positions of trust with tendencies to abuse children.

Others have observed that 'victims' now play a greater part in thinking about crime and welfare than ever before (Garland, 2001). In a globalized world, life is more and more risky and parents have become more aware of and more concerned about the dangers for children of being victimized or abused, and are more ready to regulate children's lives to protect them. 'Child abuse is real but it is equally a device for constituting a reality' (Jenks, 1996, p. 95). In recent years, younger children have been drawn into the justice system through policies designed to tackle antisocial behaviour and other 'incivilities' as more aspects of their behaviour come under scrutiny as potentially problematic. There is, as is shown in Chapter 5, some evidence that public perceptions about dangerous children and about dangers to children are at odds with trends in violent crime and with children's experiences of victimization.

Summary

- Defining violence is not straightforward because what is considered to be violent changes over time, across cultures, according to context and according to whose voices matter in defining what is legitimate, normalized or abuse.
- What counts as crime and as violence has been largely defined by adults so that official statistics tend to measure and report on crimes that concern adults.
- Children's experiences of violence and crime need to be understood developmentally, taking into account the dependency and power relationships that often exist between the perpetrator and victim.
- Risks of abuse and victimization for children and young people from different perpetrators vary across the life course. However, peers and known adults are more frequently perpetrators than are predatory 'strangers'.
- Information on crimes by children and young people tends to be collected separately from information on experiences of victimization, yet, as will be shown in later chapters, bullying research suggests that young people do not always fit neatly into the distinct groups of being either a victim or a perpetrator. Practitioners need to be alert to the overlapping aspects of experiences of violence and abuse.

Further reading

DSCF (2010) *Working Together to Safeguard Children and Young People*. London: DSCF.

This is the government guidance on child protection, prior to revision. The publication provides definitions of different types of child abuse, violence, neglect and exploitation, and explains the responsibilities of different statutory and community services.

Gordon, L .(1989) *Heroes of Their Own Lives* London: Virago.

Provides a detailed history of the development of interventions against family violence from 1860 to 1960. The research is based on social work case records on child abuse, neglect, domestic violence and incest drawn for three agencies in Boston, USA.

Garland, D. (2001) *The Culture of Control*. Oxford: Oxford University Press.

Considers how concerns about risk and victims in the context of restructuring welfare regimes have influenced the governance of self and brought a growing emphasis on responsibilization for individuals and communities.

Heywood, C. (2001) *A History of Childhood*. Oxford: Polity Press.

Charts the history of childhood in the UK, drawing upon a range of source materials.

Parton, N. (1985) *The Politics of Child Abuse*. Basingstoke: Macmillan.

Discusses the history of 'discovery' of child abuse and neglect from the nineteenth century to the mid-1980s and the political influences on the developments of policy and practice.

Research details

The British Crime Survey of Children

The British Crime Survey is an annual survey of a representative sample of adults and children living in households in England and Wales. About 37,000 adults are interviewed. The survey was extended to cover children aged 10 to 15 in 2009, when 3,661 children and young people were interviewed after their parent had completed the adult survey.

For the most recent survey see Chaplin, R., Flatley, J. and Smith, K. (2011) *Crime in England and Wales 2010–11*, London: Home Office (www.homeoffice.gov.uk).

Child Abuse and Neglect in the UK Today

This was a household survey of a representative sample of the UK population of families with children and young people aged under 25. The research was conducted for the NSPCC in 2009. Some 6,196 interviews about childhood experiences of maltreatment and victimization were collected from parents reporting for children aged under 11, from children and young people aged

11 to 17 and from young adults aged 18 to 24 using the standard victimization survey methods of Computer Assisted Self Interviewing (CASI), and Audio-CASI (A-CASI) where sensitive questions are asked and answered as privately as possible on a laptop computer, young people hearing questions privately through headphones. Some 2,160 interviews were completed with caregivers of children aged 0 to 10 years, 2,275 with young people aged 11 to 17 years and their primary caregivers and 1,761 with young adults aged 18 to 24 years. The research used evaluated measures of victimization and its impact, taking into account the impact on mental health as well as controlling for other experiences of adversity.

For further information see Radford, L., Corral, S., Bradley, C. Fisher, H., Bassett, C., Howat, N. and Collishaw, S. (2011) *Child Abuse and Neglect in the UK Today*. London: NSPCC www.nspcc.org.uk/childstudy.

Note

1 The tragic and brutal killing of baby Peter Connelly by his mother's sex offender boyfriend in 2007 created a surge of public debate about social workers' and doctors' apparent inability to effectively protect children. Seventeen-month-old Peter Connelly received over 50 injuries and was seen 60 times by professionals over the eight-month period of monitoring by social services that preceded his death. He died with injuries that included a broken back, eight fractured ribs, torn-off finger-nails, multiple bruising and a broken tooth, in the London borough of Haringey, the same authority where, seven years previously, 8-year-old Victoria Climbie was starved to death and tortured by her 'aunt'.

Part 2

An Interdisciplinary Overview of Recent Research and Scholarship

Why Are Some Children Violent?

Introduction and key questions

Areas of social policy such as criminal justice and child protection are politically charged and host to a wide range of rival theoretical and ideological approaches seeking to explain and deal with violence and crime. Children who break the law, especially those who are violent, challenge adult idealized views of childhood innocence (James and James, 2004). This chapter will consider how violence in childhood is explained, looking at the development of theories about the causes and consequences of violence from literature on aggression, deviancy and crime. A wide range of scholarship exists but some simplification and categorization of approaches will be necessary to aid analysis.

Questions considered in this chapter will be:

- How much violence is committed by children and young people?
- What are the circumstances and characteristics of young offenders?
- How has violence in childhood been explained and understood?

Theoretical analyses aimed at understanding why children might use violence have highlighted a bundle of other related questions we need to consider:

- Do the roots of violent crime lie in childhood?
- Are children naturally aggressive?
- Are boys more violent than are girls?
- Is childhood aggression and offending mostly 'trivial'?
- Do most children grow out of aggressive behaviour in the same way that they might grow out of crime, or do aggressive children grow into violent adults?
- Does violence beget violence, so that children with violent parents grow into violent adults?
- To what extent do peers and gangs influence children and young people to commit crimes and acts of violence?
- Are children dangerous or are they over regulated?

How much violence is committed by children and young people?

Media reports on antisocial drunken youths, lager ladettes in Guildford high street, children in gangs and young people with nowhere to play hanging about on the streets and dubbed 'feral children' (Frean, 2008) give the impression that Britain is well and truly 'broken'. How much of the widely reported 'misbehaviour' and incivilities of children and young people is actually violent crime, and is this increasing? Is childhood aggression and offending mostly 'trivial'?

Example of research

Between 2003 to 2007 the Home Office conducted an annual survey of young people's (10 to 25 years) self-reported experiences of crime. The surveys found that the majority of young people (78% in 2006) had not committed any of the 20 core offences in the past 12 months. Those who did break the law did so infrequently and committed relatively trivial offences. In the 2006 survey 22

⇨

per cent had committed at least one of the 20 core offences in the past 12 months, the most commonly reported offences being assault (12%) and thefts (12%). Half (50%) of those who had committed any offence in the previous 12 months had also been victims of a personal crime in the same time period compared to about one-fifth (19%) of those who had not committed any offence. Twenty-two per cent of young people had committed at least one type of anti social behaviour in the past 12 months, the most frequent being noisy or rude in public (13%) and behaving in a way likely to cause a neighbour to complain (11%). The peak age for offending was between ages 14 and 17, with a high overlap between this and anti social behaviour which peaked earlier at ages 14 to 15. Males were found to be more likely to offend and commit antisocial behaviour than females. Four per cent of 10- to 25-year-olds were prolific offenders responsible for 32 per cent of all offences. Prolific offenders begin offending at an earlier age, at 12.4 years.

Sources: Hales *et al.*, (2009); Roe and Ashe, (2008)

Findings from research provide a different picture of childhood crime to that given by the media. Most children and young people are law-abiding. Those who do break the law do so infrequently and commit relatively minor offences. Crime is strongly associated with age and proportionately more offenders are under age 25. One-third of young offenders convicted or cautioned are under age 21 (DCSF, 2009). Fifty-three per cent of offenders responsible for violent crimes are aged between 16 and 24, 12 per cent are under age 16 (Flatley *et al.*, 2010). Rates of offending decline after age 17, as research shows, that young people grow out of crime (Rutherford, 1992). Females comprise 22 per cent of offenders sentenced by the courts and 5 per cent of the prison population. The criminal offence most frequently committed by girls in England and Wales is theft or handling stolen goods (Ministry of Justice, 2010a). Nine out of ten (91%) offenders involved in violent crimes are males (Flatley *et al.*, 2010). Most of the violence reported to the British Crime Survey (BCS) and recorded by the police results in no injury (51 per cent of violence reported to BCS and 46 per cent of violence recorded by the police result in injury) or in injuries that are minor (BCS—31 per cent bruising or black eye, 11 per cent scratches) (Flatley *et al.*, 2010).

In England and Wales no child can be found guilty of a crime below age 10, and between 10 and 18 young people are subject to juvenile courts. In other jurisdictions the age of criminal responsibility ranges from 8 (Scotland) to 18 (Belgium and Luxembourg). In the UK we have more, and younger, children under the spotlight of crime and antisocial behaviour policies. Juvenile offenders in England can be detained from age 12 and for serious crimes at the age of 10. England and Wales have particularly high rates of youth crime, with more young people in custody than other European countries (besides Turkey). Although there has been a recent downward trend, the level of imprisonment for 14- to 17-year-olds is still double that in the early 1990s. 2,209 under-18s were in custody in 2010 (2,089 boys and 120 girls) (Natale, 2010).

As with children's experiences of victimization (Chapter 1) historically there have been rediscoveries of juvenile crime and violence (Pearson, 1983). At present, public perceptions of levels of violent crime do not match rates measured by self-report (the BCS) or incidents recorded by the police. The majority of adults (66%) think that crime is increasing and that lax parenting is a strong factor influencing levels of crime (Flately *et al.*, 2010). However, BCS and police data show a decline in all crimes of 9 per cent and 8 per cent respectively comparing 2009 to 2010 with 2008–2009. For violent crime, BCS data show a decline of 50 per cent since the peak in 1995 (Flatley *et al.*, 2010). Crimes by young people are similarly declining, according to police data. From 2001 to 2008/9 there was a fall in 10- to 17-year-olds in England receiving their first reprimand, warning or conviction. The rate of young people per 100,000 aged 10–17 receiving their first reprimand, warning or conviction in England fell to 1,472 in 2008 to 2009, which is a decrease of 20.7 per cent from a rate of 1,857 in 2007 to 2008 (DCSF, 2009).

As the research on page 31 shows, there is an overlap between offending and victimization, especially for violence. Those who are violent towards others experience a lot of violence themselves. Indeed, as was shown in Chapter 1, children and young people experience more violence than they perpetrate, but the justice system has been preoccupied with juvenile offending and has given less attention to children as victims. This can be seen from the historical preoccupations within criminology where most interest has centred on youth crime in public places and on the streets, or on severe forms of violent or sexual offending. Only recently has abuse in young people's intimate relationships been included (Barter *et al.*, 2009). Bullying is rarely considered in broader discussions of children's violence, despite the research presented in Chapter 1 that shows victimization by peers to be the most frequent victimization experience children and young people report (Finkelhor *et al.*, 2009; Radford *et al.*, 2011).

Characteristics and circumstances of young offenders

Research that looked at the characteristics of 300 young offenders in custody and in the community found that:

- Seventy-seven per cent were male.
- While eighty-three per cent were white British, young people from ethnic minorities were over-represented.
- Seventy-four per cent no longer lived with both biological parents.
- Thirty-seven per cent had previously been in 'care'.
- Seventy-seven per cent had parents in manual employment.
- One in five had an IQ below 70, meeting the criteria for learning disability; one in three had a borderline learning disability.
- The mean reading age of young offenders was 11.3 years, significantly below the mean age of 15.7 years.
- Almost one in ten had self-harmed in the past month.
- One in ten reported anxiety or post-traumatic stress symptoms.
- Eleven per cent had an alcohol problem.
- Twenty per cent had drug problems.
- There were no significant differences between male and female young offenders apart from in the area of mental health. Females were more likely to be depressed, self-harm or to have post-traumatic stress.
- The needs of the young people were mostly unmet; few had any intervention to help them overcome their problems.

(Chitsabesan *et al.*, 2006)

A large minority of those who do commit offences and have criminal sanctions are likely to re-offend: 37.3 per cent of young offenders re-offend within a year (Ministry of Justice, 2010b). Prolific young offenders are young people who have lived with a high level of poverty, disadvantage and abuse. Maltreatment in childhood affects boys and girls as offenders but it has a greater impact on subsequent delinquency and violence by females than it has on males (Makarios, 2007). Widom (2000) conducted a longitudinal study of physically and sexually abused and neglected boys and girls aged birth to 11, who were matched with a control group and studied into young adulthood. Girls who had been abused or neglected in childhood were twice as likely to be arrested while adolescents, twice as likely to be arrested as adults and 2.4 times more likely to be arrested for violent crimes, than were non-abused and neglected girls. However, 70 per cent of the girls in the abused or neglected sample did not go on to offend. This suggests that although abuse or neglect may increase the likelihood of girls taking part in crime, this is not inevitable.

How has children's violence been explained and understood?

Theory and research on children and violence has roots in different academic disciplines and there seem to be few texts in existence that have brought these together. Criminology has produced a wealth of different approaches that aim to explain criminal behaviour (why individuals deviate or conform) and/ or the processes of criminalization (what counts as criminal and what gets normalized). Clinicians working as researchers and practitioners, mostly in mental health, have investigated violent and abusive behaviour as 'pathologies', 'perversions', 'conduct disorders' and other individual abnormalities. Child development perspectives have emphasized aggression in stages of childhood development. Reviewing comprehensively all this literature is beyond the scope of this short text and readers are advised to refer to the texts recommended at the end of this chapter for further information. In this section the aim will be to draw from the rich and diverse literature four (not mutually exclusive) recurrent themes:

1 the biology of violence;
2 parenting and socialization;
3 peers, subcultures and boys' gangs;
4 growing into and out of crime.

These themes are relevant to later discussion of policy and practice, particularly in relation to the 'public health approach' towards violence reduction which has been influential in crime prevention thinking in the USA and UK in the past ten years (McVeigh *et al.*, 2005). This will be discussed in more detail in later chapters, so a brief introduction is all that is necessary here. This approach, promoted by global organizations such as the World Health Organization, takes an epidemiological, population-based disease control approach to preventing violence. This involves empirically researching the nature and scale of the problem in a community and evaluating, on a dose-response randomized trial basis, which interventions are most effective in violence reduction (Krug *et al.*, 2002). It has been a widely employed approach to crime control policies aimed at targeting communities and neighbourhoods and families that are perceived as being 'high risk' of violence and antisocial behaviour.

It's in their genes – the biology of violence

The biology of violence

Biosocial theory: This theory considers that certain biological anomalies or physical disabilities may make some individuals more prone to violence. These can stem from nutritional deficiencies, hormonal influences, allergies or exposure to environmental contaminants, or may arise from neuro-physical conditions, such as fetal alcohol syndrome, brain dysfunction, injury or chemistry, genetics or evolution. According to many of these sub-theories, the studied condition leads to difficulties in controlling violent impulses when under stress and has its origins in circumstances often associated with poverty or dysfunctional families.

(MuCurty and Curling, 2008)

Early scientific studies of crime developed in the nineteenth century and were 'positivist'. Positivism in criminology has three characteristics:

- The criminal is a specific type of person, who can be classified by certain characteristics.
- The criminal is different to other people and these differences can be listed to help with identification of criminal types.
- The criminal is driven to crime by factors outside his or her control so crime is determined by things such as biology, nature or inherent weakness.

(Carrabine *et al.*, 2004)

Cesare Lombroso, often cited as an early pioneer in the study of crime, applied Darwin's ideas about evolution and natural selection to his research into the physical features of criminal, 'atavistic', men, deemed to be lower down the evolutionary scale and more like apes than humans (Lombroso, 1876). Biology has been studied in inherited factors, in hereditary factors that may change during the life course in response to the environment and finally as factors that originate in the environment, but affect a person's biology or bodily influences. Heavily criticized by social scientists and feminists in the 1970s to 1980s as determinist, biological perspectives have gained more interest as a result of recent developments in medicine, genetics and brain sciences.

This area of research has looked extensively at the questions 'Do the roots of violent crime lie in childhood?, 'Are children naturally aggressive?' and 'Are boys more violent than girls?' Research on aggression in animals and a long history of twin and adoption studies have explored the genetic/inherited proneness to violence, particularly in juveniles (Mednick *et al.*, 1984). Twin studies tend to show a greater similarity in criminal behaviour for identical compared with non-identical twins; however, it is not always possible to disentangle the influence of environment from influences of hereditry in these studies (Vold *et al.*, 2002). Hormones have also been studied to explain male aggression. Hormones have been shown to affect animal behaviour and aggression. For example, castrated male mice are less aggressive than non-castrated mice. In humans however, research studies of the male hormone testosterone and violent crime show mixed results and beg questions about causality. Violent individuals may have higher levels of testosterone as a response to engaging in violent behaviour, rather than the testosterone causing or precipitating the aggression (Radford, 2004).

Recent biological approaches are much more likely to acknowledge that the factors influencing violence and aggression are complex and not determined by one hereditary deterministic factor. Genetic, neurophysiological and neurochemical factors, combined with upbringing and social and environmental variables, can create within an individual a propensity towards violent behaviour. Identifying this propensity has implications for how a society is able to manage the risk of violence and crime.

Research on brain anatomy and behaviour brings together genetics, family factors and environment to investigate abnormalities caused by poor development, abuse, trauma or accident, identifying regions in the brain linked with emotions and violent behaviour. By itself, a brain lesion is unlikely to cause violent behaviour. Indeed, most people with brain damage are not violent. Dysfunctions in the brain as a result of injury or abnormality, especially to areas such as the limbic system,[1] the amygdala[2] and frontal lobes,[3] combined with, aggravated by or resulting in a chemical or hormonal under/overload are however said to be one of the factors contributing to a propensity for violence.

Nuerotransmitters are the chemicals that allow the transmission of electrical impulses in the brain, enabling the processing of information. Research has explored three neurotransmitters thought to be associated with anti social behaviour—serotonin, dopamine and noradrenaline (known as norepinephrine in the USA). Serotonin is said to act as an inhibiter to aggressive impulses, putting the brakes on violent urges fuelled by too much of the male sex hormone testosterone. Drugs and alcohol can have an aggravating impact by lowering serotonin levels in the brain, thereby 'loosening the brakes' on aggression. From this perspective children inherit a genetic propensity to violence from parents activated/aggravated by the effects of childhood abuse on the developing brain.

Rutter's work on the development of antisocial behaviour in children has been influential (1998). Rutter has argued that psychobiological reactivity and genetic factors play a key role in determining individual differences between children's coping abilities and may explain why children in the same family situation will react differently (Rutter, 1996). It has been argued that exposure to violence as a child could lead to neurophysiological changes and developmental brain damage that increase a person's risk of becoming violent in adult life. Post-traumatic stress disorder (PTSD) is thought to have a long-lasting effect on neurotransmitter functions including higher levels of adrenaline, noradrenaline and glucocorticoids and lower levels of serotonin. These neurotransmitter changes are claimed to underlie the behavioural symptoms of PTSD. In children PTSD symptoms such as high arousal and difficulty in concentrating could interfere with learning and development. Over time, it is argued, PTSD could lead to difficulties in brain development and neurophysiological traumatic stress responses, and increased risk of aggression and depression.

While the new biological explanations are less deterministic and more likely to consider the interaction between hereditary, hormonal or neurological factors and environmental factors, the relative importance of biological and environmental factors in influencing violence and aggression in children is not agreed (Klahr *et al.*, 2011).

Reflections on the theory and the research

What are the implications of biological explanations of violence and aggression for preventing and responding to violence in childhood?

Are biological explanations applicable to 'white-collar crimes', such as banking fraud, committed by wealthy adults? Why are biological explanations most commonly applied to violence and antisocial behaviour?

Parenting and socialization

Does violence beget violence, so that children with violent parents grow into violent adults?

In post-war Britain John Bowlby's theory of attachment, based on the idea that an affective bond between an infant and carer was essential for survival and healthy development, was influential (Bowlby, 1988). Bowlby's ideas contributed to the promotion of the post-war male breadwinner family ideal, with stay-at-home mothers and wage-earning fathers seen as the best environment in which to raise children (this will be discussed further in Chapter 4). The family was seen to be the core agency for transmitting social values and behaviour, and as a result was central in theories of crime. In more recent policy debates, problems arising in low-income, single-parent families living in social housing communities with out-of-control children and youth have become targets of a range of family-focused parenting and antisocial behaviour initiatives (further discussed in Chapters 5 and 6).

Socialization and psychological theories view aggression as learnt in families or passed on by learning from generation to generation, rather than being inherited or passed on genetically. Early research established that hostile parents, or those who are indifferent, are more likely to produce delinquent children (Glueck and Glueck, 1950). In social learning theories children are believed to imitate parental behaviour (Bandura, 1973). Children are also thought to grow into violent or criminal adults because they have had a family background that failed in socialization, failing to curb innate tendencies in human beings to pursue immediate gratification through the practice of social and self-control.

Research findings

Travis Hirschi's writings on control have been important in criminology. Rather than centring attention on the minority of deviants and law-breakers, Hirschi wanted to explain why most people conform. He hypothesized that those who have strong bonds with their parents or schools, and commitment, a stake in conformity and a belief that rules should be obeyed, are least likely to commit violent offences and risk causing upset, disapproval or disappointment among the people whom they value. Crime occurs when social bonds, based on attachments to parents, school and others, are weak. Hirschi tested his theory on boys in American schools and found some confirmation (Hirschi, 1969).

Social control theory has also been adapted to explain gender differences in violence and criminality. Frances Heidensohn, for example, explained the lower rates of criminality and higher level of conformity among females by arguing that girls and women are 'over-controlled' by the family, motherhood, community, as well as within wider social institutions and social policy. On this perspective, females are far more likely than males to have a stake in conformity and to be expected to conform. Girls and women who step outside expected patterns of behaviour by, for example, committing acts of violence are heavily sanctioned (Heidensohn, 1985).

Gottfredson and Hirschi's general theory of crime shifted the emphasis from broader community and social pressures on conformity towards the inner factors of an individual's ability to exert self-control (Gottfredson and Hirschi, 1990). The family, however, still played a crucial role in the development of self-control. It was argued that children develop self-control if their parents, within the first decade of the child's life, set clear rules, monitor their behaviour, recognize rule violations, and sanction such violations consistently. Lack of self-control means an individual is more likely to pursue immediate gratification and crime, to act impulsively, risk-take, be bad-tempered, insensitive to the suffering of others, lack persistence and avoid difficult tasks or tasks that involve concentration (Rebellon *et al.*, 2008).

The idea that the family is the root source of good and evil has helped inspire a substantial research literature on the intergenerational transmission of violence which drew heavily on social learning, socialization, social control and self-control approaches. Researchers have attempted to show that mothers who lack self-control are more likely to have delinquent children (Nofziger, 2009). Males exposed to family violence and inconsistent physical punishment have been found to show higher rates of aggression and violence in relationships as adults (Straus and Smith, 1990). Young people who have been maltreated were more likely to engage in risky behaviour and the lifestyle risks associated with crime (Wilson and Spatz-Widom, 2011). The intergenerational cycle of violence approach has been controversial and criticized for assuming that victimization or exposure to violence in childhood will inevitably determine aggressive behaviour in adulthood (Mullender, 1996), because as noted earlier most children who are abused in childhood do not grow up to be violent offenders. Family factors are now seen not to be solely deterministic of future behaviour but instead, as shown later in this chapter, are part of the overall bundle of risks and protective factors that might increase or decrease the likelihood of offending.

Reflections on the research

What are the policy and practice implications of the intergenerational cycle of violence perspective for preventing and responding to violence in childhood?

Peers, subcultures and boys' gangs

To what extent do peers and gangs influence children and young people to commit crimes and acts of violence?

Does the UK have a problem with gang violence?

Violent knife offending has tended to mirror trends in overall violent crime, which rose sharply in the 1970s and 1980s but has fallen since the mid-1990s. However, the number of knife homicides increased by over a quarter between 2005/6 and 2006/7; there also appeared to be a rise in other serious knife violence during this year. The high levels of knife violence since 2006 appear to be the result of an increase in street violence between groups of young people who are sometimes referred to as 'gangs' Most young people do not carry knives; only 4 per cent living in high-risk areas have ever done so and those who do carry knives say they do so for 'protection', having been victimized themselves.

(House of Commons Home Affairs Committee Knife Crime Seventh Report of Session 2008–09 HC 112–1 Home Office London)

UK gang members are:

- predominantly male
- aged between 12 and 19 and getting younger;
- concentrated in poor urban areas characterized by social housing;
- have ethnicity that reflects the local population;
- have low trust in police and adults as their protectors;
- often young people who are excluded from school;
- engaged in prolific offending, drug dealing, violence and rape;
- more likely to grow up in single-parent families, living with domestic violence and lack a positive role model.

The issue of 'territoriality' is a key factor in why some young people felt the need for protection. Others carry knives to get 'respect', gain 'street cred' or to scare others.

(Adapted from *Dying to Belong: An In Depth Review of Street Gangs in Britain* (2009) Simon Antropus London Centre for Social Justice)

The role of peers in influencing behaviour has already been noted with reference to social control. The post-war period brought changes in mass consumption and youth subcultures emerged that were based on distinct consumer-oriented identities: teds, mods, rockers, etc. In the 1960s style became important and a way for young people to identify as part of a group that was against the mainstream. Criminology entered a radical phase and interest shifted away from individual behaviour towards the processes of criminalization, with a greater tendency to view society and social inequalities as at the roots of juvenile crime.

Three themes can be identified in the criminological research on peers and the community:

- *Feeling outside*—Those with friends or relatives who offend are more likely to also engage in law-breaking. Young people turn to crime because they are disillusioned or feel they are alienated and outside of the mainstream (suffer from a lack of norms of behaviour or anomie), or suffer from strain as a result of thwarted goals and seek alternative routes to achieve esteem.
- *Subculture or rebellion*—Young people form subgroups or criminal gangs as acts of rebellion against mainstream values or to conform to the values of oppositional and alternative criminal subcultures.
- *Social disorganization*—The communities and neighbourhoods in which young people live provide fertile ground for crime and violence by presenting opportunities and peer support for crime and violence, lack of alternatives as a result of social exclusion and inequality and lack of community sanctions.

Research from the USA by Cohen (1955) and Cloward and Ohlin (1960) was influential in directing attention to gangs and deviant subcultures of boys as a source of criminal activity, mostly looking at street crimes and theft. The subcultural theorists highlighted how feelings of inequality, being outside of or excluded from the mainstream, can interact with norms of behaviour learned through associations with peers and contribute to crime or violence if opportunities for this exist in communities.

Theory example—Gangs, subcultures and crime

In subculture theory juvenile crime was seen as a resistance or response by young people to their disillusion with the consumer capitalist society that emerged in the 1960s. For example, Cloward and Ohlin explained working-class boys' criminality

⇨

Theory example—Gangs, subcultures and crime—Cont'd

on the basis of anomie, learning about crime from peers and having a different opportunity structure in a community that enabled crime to occur. Cloward and Ohlin argued that working-class boys saw their legitimate opportunities for success being blocked as a result of class bias. They argued that three types of illegal opportunity could result in response to this, depending on what opportunities were available—criminal, conflict and retreatist. A criminal gang would only emerge as an option if opportunities to handle and deal with stolen goods existed and were tolerated in the neighbourhood. Conflict gangs would arise if there were no opportunities for criminal activities and success was sought by working-class boys demonstrating toughness in gangs based on territorial or identity-related violence. The third type of subcultural gang was retreatist or drug oriented and likely to emerge in neighbourhoods where drugs could be obtained. The solution to the strain caused by not achieving the capitalist ideal would be sought in a retreat or blocking out of the perceived unfairness of life by the use of drugs.

(Cloward and Ohlin, 1960)

Crime is more prevalent in urban areas but rates of crime differ between cities and different neighbourhoods. Neighbourhoods with high residential mobility, ethnic heterogenity and low economic status tend to have higher crime rates. Social disorganization (Weijers *et al.*, 2009) and subcultural theories propose that such neighbourhoods lack conventional institutions of social control, such as stable families, schools, churches, etc., and are weak and unable to regulate the behaviour of the neighbourhood's residents.

Reflections on the theory and research
Activity

Try to apply biological, social control and subcultural approaches to explain the characteristics of young offenders outlined in the research box on page 33.
What are the advantages and limitations of each approach?

Individual approaches such as biological and self-control perspectives emphasize personal factors that influence crime while subcultural perspectives highlighted inequality, social exclusion, opportunity and, to varying degrees, choices. Focusing on individual or family factors supports policies that target behaviour and family problems while focusing also on social inequalities and opportunities for crime in a neighbourhood support community-focused interventions that might provide different opportunities or alternatives to crime.

The bulk of the work on deviancy subcultures in the UK in the 1970s focused on young, white, working-class males and there was little said about how crime or deviancy in gangs or subcultures related to girls or young people from ethnic minorities. The creation of new crimes such as 'mugging', which the media portrayed as predominantly black male youth crime, brought greater awareness of the over-policing experienced by ethnic minorities and a greater interest in the police role in the criminalization of young black males (Hall *et al.*, 1980). Feminist criminologists also noted the lack of attention given to gender. Although the majority of offenders in contact with the criminal justice system are from low-income families, arguments about poverty and inequality determining crime cannot explain well why proportionately more females suffer poverty yet fewer resort to crime or join violent gangs (Carlen, 1988).

By the 1980s and 1990s criminology had developed a substantial interest in research on gender, sexuality, identity, ethnicity and the masculinity of gangs and young offending, often from a social constructionist perspective.

Theory example: A social constructionist approach

Social constructionism is an approach to theory that emphasizes the socially created nature of social life, where human beings actively create, interpret and shape social life. It is usually contrasted with determinism, theories that view human beings driven in turn by their biology or social life as driven by the fundamental principles of an economy and the inequalities associated with it. The Australian sociologist Connell took a social constructionist approach to argue that gender, being 'male' or female', is not a biological given but a historically, socially and culturally situated accomplishment, achieved in the everyday performance of masculinity or femininity. Societies have a range of socially constructed masculinities but there exists a hegemonic (dominant) masculinity towards which men are expected to strive and against which alternative subordinated masculinities (such as being gay or a boy or not successful) are measured. Hegemonic masculinity emphasizes authority, control, competitive individualism, independence, aggressiveness and capacity for violence. In their everyday interactions Connell argued that men use the resources available to them to show they are manly and they sanction and oppress subordinate masculinities.

Theory example: Masculinity, violence and crime

Messerschmidt (1993) explored the relationship between masculinity and crime to try to understand how males and females and young people of different ethnicities may have different experiences of crime and violence. Messerschmidt argued that different masculinities can result in different patterns of crime. Members of poor or minority ethnic groups seek different ways of asserting gender, as they are less able to achieve this in economic and professional success. Boys resort to oppositional masculinities where respect is often gained through the subordination of girls and showing them 'who is boss'. Violence is a means for men to demonstrate their own masculinity, targeting other men and women in displays of masculine toughness. Messerschmidt also applied this thinking about hegemonic masculinity to female gangs where criminal behaviour was seen as a particular way of challenging femininity and creating new ways of performing femininity for socially disadvantaged girls.

Reflections on the theory

Consider the possible policy options that might be proposed by taking a social constructionist approach to explain the role of masculinity and femininity in young people's gang membership.

Growing into and out of crime

Do most children grow out of aggressive behaviour in the same way that they might grow out of crime, or do aggressive children grow into violent adults?

Key developmental stages

- *Infancy*: attachment, assistance in regulation of bodily states, emotional regulation.
- *Toddlerhood*: development of symbolic representation and further self-other differentiation, problem-solving, pride, mastery, motivation.
- *Pre-school*: development of self-control, use of language to regulate impulses, emotions, store information, predict and make sense of the world, development of verbally mediated or semantic memory, gender identity, development of social relationships beyond immediate family and generalization of expectations about relationships, moral reasoning.

⇨

- *Latency age*: peer relationships, adaptation to school environment, moral reasoning.
- *Adolescence*: renegotiation of family roles, identity issues—sexuality, future orientation, peer acceptance, ethnicity, moral reasoning.
- *Young adults*: continued differentiation from family, refinement and integration of identity with particular focus on occupational choice and intimate partners, moral reasoning.

(Barlow and Schrader-McMillan, 2010, p. 33)

Child development theories conceptualize childhood as having key developmental periods, each being associated with developmental tasks—forming a secure attachment with the primary caregiver in early infancy, developing a sense of self in toddlerhood and self-control of impulses and emotions in pre-school years. The child's developmental process can be 'derailed' at various stages and early disruptions are seen to influence later developmental tasks. For example, a parent's hostility or rejection of the toddler's seeking of affection or need for comfort can affect the child's security, self-worth and trust in other people. Aggression is seen to be part of this developmental process with the majority of young children aged 17 months or so using aggression to resolve conflict, often over possessions, and learning alternative methods to resolve conflict using language and negotiation before they start school (Tremblay and Nagin, 2004).

Developmental criminology has similarly studied young people's crime by looking at how different factors have different effects at different stages in the life course. It has arguably contributed the most to understanding pathways into crime and violent or abusive behaviour, recognizing that crime is complex and has multiple causes. The focus of the work has been very much on trying to explain the most severe and unusual types of persistent violent conduct. Well-known examples of these longitudinal and prospective studies are the Cambridge Study in Delinquent Development which tracked a sample of 411 males living in South London from age 8 to 50 (Farrington *et al.*, 2006) and the Edinburgh Study of Youth Transitions and Crime, conducted among young people attending certain schools, starting at the end of the 1990s (McAra and McVie, 2007), and more recently prospective, longitudinal research in Switzerland looking at the development of aggression in a sample of 1,675 primary school children (Eisner and Ribeaud, 2010).

Developmental criminology is concerned with three main issues:

- the development of offending and antisocial behaviour;
- risk factors at different ages;
- the effects of life events on the course of development.

In studying offending, efforts are made to study age of onset and different patterns of offending at different ages, life course persistence and desistance in offending, and the processes of graduating from hyperactivity to conduct disorder and then to crime. Risk factors explored at different ages include biological, individual, family, peer, school, neighbourhood and situational factors. A key finding to emerge from the work is that young people who begin offending at an early age (early onset offenders) are much more likely to persist in chronic and violent offending as adults.

The Cambridge Study in Delinquent Development which started in 1961/2 to research the family backgrounds and criminal behaviour of South London boys over time up until 2004 (Farrington *et al.*, 2006) and subsequent research (reviewed by Wong *et al.*, 2010) has proposed a number of risk factors that predict offending for males and females. These individual, family, school and peer-related factors are shown in Table 2.1.

Table 2.1 Risk factors for offending

1 Individual risk factors

Unique factors for females	Shared risk factors	Unique factors for males
High number of life events	Victimization	Birth complications
Disobedience	Being harassed by an adult	Psychological well-being
High self-esteem	Low self-control	
Depression	Aggression	
Suicidal behaviour	Low IQ	
	Low self-esteem	
	Being unashamed towards parents, friends and teachers	
	Positive attitude towards delinquency	
	Substance abuse	

2 Family factors

Unique factors for females	Shared risk factors	Unique factors for males
Maternal parenting style	Inadequate parenting (father or both parents)	High parental knowledge about friends
Low child disclosure	Paternal parenting style	Convicted mother
Being seldom at home	Overall parental monitoring	Single parenthood
Physical abuse by parents	Decreasing parental monitoring	
Low parental trust	Low involvement of parents in school	
Low maternal support	Small number of rules at home	
Low-quality mother–child relationship	Harsh discipline	
	Low parental warmth	
	Conflicts within family	
	Low-quality father–child relationship	
	Convicted father	
	Delinquent sibling	
	Living in a disadvantaged neighbourhood	

3 School risk factors

Unique factors for females	Shared risk factors	Unique factors for males
Low-quality relationship with teachers	Low school commitment	Low school achievement

4 Peer risk factors

Unique factors for females	Shared risk factors	Unique factors for males
Extent of delinquency of friends	Having delinquent friends	
	Having negative friends	
	Problematic youth group membership	
	Having a romantic partner	
	Many activities with friends	
	Having friends disliked by parents	

Source: Adapted from Wong *et al.*, (2010)

Short-term, situational risk factors interact with the accumulation of these longer term risk factors and in the absence of protective factors it is observed that delinquency is more likely. Short-term risk factors include the opportunity to offend presented by the situation, some situations being more conducive to offending than others (e.g. where there is no surveillance), the presence of co-offenders, little or no risk of being caught and lack of guardianship.

The life course studies brought an explosion of research on violent and sexual offences by children and young people. Moffit's study in New Zealand identified life course persistent and adolescent onset delinquent and violent offenders (Moffit, 1993; Moffit *et al.*, 2002). What is most interesting about these works is that they take into account the very large number of young people who commit only one or two offences in adolescence and then desist, and do not follow a pathway into violence in adulthood. Desistance is linked to lifestyle changes, particularly having pro-social sources of informal social control, most often gained by acquiring a stable partner relationship, obtaining suitable employment and moving away from criminal friends. Also important is the individual's own decision to desist (Farrall *et al.*, 2010). For Moffit *et al.*, the life course persistent young offenders tend to be more anti social and delinquent, begin criminality at a younger age and have different developmental antecedents. Their families have poorer mental health and are of low socioeconomic status; the youth tend to have challenging neurological developments (Moffitt *et al.*, 2002), and they are typically raised in a crimo-genic environment with inadequate parenting. Adolescent onset delinquents, those who tend not to persist in violent delinquency, are not distinguished by these features.

Research example: Victim to victimizer

Burton and colleagues (2011) studied the offender pathways of 325 incarcerated adolescent male sex offenders, ranging in age from 12 to 19. Fifty-five per cent had themselves been sexually abused during childhood. The researchers compared the developmental antecedents (trauma, family characteristics, exposure to pornography, personality factors) and behavioural characteristics of the victimized and the non-victimized sex offenders to test whether the history and severity of a young person's own experiences of sexual abuse influenced the subsequent abusive behaviour and its severity. Sexually victimized child sex offenders had more adverse

⇨

developmental antecedents than did non-sexually victimized offenders. They not only had more experiences of childhood victimization than the non-victimized juvenile sex offenders, they were more likely to have witnessed criminality at home or in their communities and were more likely to have exposure to pornography before age 10. The victimized sex offenders were found to start abuse at a younger age (11.7 years compared with 13.3 years), were more likely to commit incest, had higher numbers of reported victims, were more likely to abuse males, to commit more serious offences and to use pornography. The victimized group had more traumatic childhoods, elevated scores on personality measures, lived in more crimogenic environments and exhibited more antisocial behaviours, which started younger and lasted longer than behaviours exhibited by the non-victimized sex offenders. Moffit's categorization of early onset, adolescent onset and life course persistent offending was applied to the sex offender research to identify early onset (paraphilic) offenders who abuse children, adolescent onset (non-paraphilic) offenders who sexually abuse adults and peers, and life course persistent offenders. The researchers concluded that the victimized offenders were best understood as life course persistent and early onset offenders while the non-sexually victimized offenders showed more adolescent limited behaviour patterns, being delinquent youth who commit sexual offences.

Reflections on the research

What conclusions can be drawn from this research for assessment and treatment of young people with sexually harmful behaviour?

The life course pathways research brought together criminology, biological, developmental, family and community/environmental factors to focus attention on empirical research and treatment that aimed to identify the characteristics of early onset offenders among an increasingly young sector of the child population (Hickey *et al.*, 2006).

The deviant and the normalized

Hackett applied the notion of a continuum to consider developmental pathways towards persistent sexually harmful behaviour (Hackett, 2010) (Table 2.2).

The continuum helps to distinguish between abusive and problematic sexual behaviour. Sexually abusive behaviour is where there is an element of manipulation and the target is unable to give informed consent. Problematic sexually harmful behaviour does not include this element of victimization but

Table 2.2 Hackett's continuum of children's and young people's sexual behaviour

Normal	Inappropriate	Problematic	Abusive	Violent
Developmentally expected	Single incidences of inappropriate sexual behaviour	Problematic and concerning behaviours	Victimizing intent or outcome	Physically violent sexual abuse
Socially acceptable	Socially acceptable behaviour within peer group	Developmentally unusual and socially unexpected	Includes misuse of power	Highly intrusive
Consensual, mutual, reciprocal	Context for behaviour may be inappropriate	No overt elements of victimization	Coercion and force to ensure victim compliance	Instrumental violence which is physiologically and/or sexually arousing to the perpetrator
Shared decision-making	Generally consensual and reciprocal	Consent issues may be unclear	Intrusive	Sadism
		May lack reciprocity or equal power	Informed consent lacking or not able to be freely given by victim	
		May include levels of compulsivity	May include elements of expressive violence	

Source: Hackett (2010), p .122.

the behaviour may interfere with the child's development, cause distress or increase the child's risk of further victimization. The continuum places sexual behaviour within a developmental context because different behaviours have different meanings at different ages or stages of development. Some sexual behaviour may be regarded as normal if the person is a preadolescent child but it would be seen as worrying behaviour for an adolescent. Other behaviour may be seen as normal for an adolescent but worrying in a preadolescent child. Both problematic and abusive behaviour are developmentally inappropriate and can cause harm or developmental damage. Hackett's continuum is helpful for practice and for highlighting the diversity of sexually harmful behaviour among children and young people.

It is important to recognize that not all violent offenders are the same and the increasing concentration of interest on high-risk, prolific violent or sexually deviant young offenders may divert attention from efforts to understand behaviours that have a harmful impact—such as intimate partner abuse, sibling violence or 'bullying'—but are blind spots in adult-led research and practice because they are normalized as being part of the everyday experiences of children.

Are children over-regulated?

Theories of violence and crime in childhood have zoned into specialized research on the few very troubled 'early onset' young offenders, yet, as will be shown in Chapter 6, social policies have increased reach into children's lives, managing and targeting children at risk or exhibiting potential antisocial tendencies. It could be argued that children are under increased surveillance as a result and parents are expected to play a greater role in protecting children from these risks, monitoring behaviour and setting controls There are areas of children's lives, their social networking, leisure and access to IT, that remain unregulated and outside parental surveillance where risks of abuse to children and the risks children present as abusers of others are more difficult to monitor.

New childhood theorists have approached child development theory somewhat sceptically, noting that the increasing categorization of childhood in stages is associated with a social construction of childhood where children are seen to lack agency, and to be developmentally dependent on and in need of guidance and surveillance by adults (James and James, 2004). While it is the case that children and young people do grow and develop their capacities and abilities in interaction with and with guidance from adults, not all will follow the same pathways and many will grow into caring, non abusive adults despite their parents.

Summary

- Crime is strongly linked with youthfulness and masculinity but the majority of children and young people are law-abiding and children are more victimized than victimizing towards others.
- Only a minority of children and young people break the law. Most offences are trivial and not repeated.

- The 4 per cent of young people who are prolific offenders have lived with a high level of poverty, disadvantage and abuse. Maltreatment in childhood has a greater impact on subsequent delinquency and violence by females than it has on males.
- A range of different approaches have developed to explain the causes of crime, violence and aggression in childhood. These vary in their focus on explaining the development of criminal behaviour, the process of criminalization and the social construction of childhood violence.
- Recent approaches in developmental criminology take a more integrated approach, tend to be less deterministic and emphasize a range of different risks and protective factors known to be associated with persistent, prolific offending.

Further reading

Barter, C. and Berridge, D. (2010) *Children Behaving Badly: Peer Violence Between Children and Young People*. London: Wiley.

A collection of research papers on violence among young people in the UK.

Hales, J., Nevill,C. Pudney, S. and Tipping, S. (2009) *Longitudinal Analysis of the Offending, Crime and Justice Survey 2003–06: Key Implications*. Research Report 19. London: Home Office.

Longitudinal analysis of self-report data on drug use, offending and antisocial behaviour by young people aged 10 to 25 based on the Offending Crime and Justice Surveys carried out between 2003 and 2006.

James, A. and James, A. (2004) *Constructing Childhood*. London: Palgrave.

Considers the social construction of childhood, including a chapter on crime.

Maguire, M., Morgan, R. and Reiner, R. (eds) (2007) *The Oxford Handbook of Criminology* 575–601. Oxford: Oxford University Press.

A comprehensive review of criminological theory and policy issues including chapters on children and crime.

Research details

Characteristics of young offenders—Roe and Ashe

Based on computer-assisted personal interviewing/self-interviewing with a panel sample of 5,353 participants aged 10 to 25, 4,554 of whom were participants who had taken part in previous waves of the Offender Crime and Justice Surveys 2003, 2004 and 2005 with an additional 799 new participants included for 2006. Twenty core offences were considered.

Roe, S. and Ashe, J. (2008), *Young People and Crime: Findings from the 2006 Offending, Crime and Justice Survey*. London: Home Office.

Characteristics of young offenders—Hales *et al.*

A longitudinal study of all the Offender Crime and Justice Surveys 2003, 2004, 2005 and 2006 to investigate prolific and persistent offenders.

Hales, J., Nevill, C. Pudney, S. and Tipping, S. (2009) *Longitudinal Analysis of the Offending, Crime and Justice Survey 2003–06: Key Implications*. Research Report 19. London: Home Office.

Sexually victimized offenders—Burton, Daly and Leibowitz

Research with 325 sexually abusive young people aged 12 to 19 from six residential facilities in the Midwest USA. The characteristics and risk factors of those who had been sexually abused themselves (55%) were compared with the sexual abuse offenders who had no prior history of sexual victimization.

Burton, D., Duty, K. and Leibowitz, G. (2011) 'Differences between sexually victimized and nonsexually victimized male adolescent sexual abusers: Developmental antecedents and behavioral comparisons.' *Journal of Child Sexual Abuse*, 20(1): 77–93.

Notes

1 The limbic system is the anatomical area of the brain thought to be involved in many aspects of emotion.
2 Placidity is thought to be linked with bilateral amygdala damage. Removal of the amygdala reduces aggression but also results in the loss of emotion. Violence is linked with abnormal electric activity in the amygdala. The rabies virus damages the amydala and rabid animals are often aggressive.
3 The frontal lobes, especially the orbitofrontal cortices, are believed to allow for the inhibition of aggression but damage is thought to result in aggression.

3 What Causes Child Maltreatment?

Introduction and key questions

This chapter will briefly consider theoretical perspectives on the causes of child abuse, drawing out, as in previous chapters, key themes that are relevant to contemporary practice and thinking in the area of childhood studies. In Chapter 1 it was shown that child abuse is prevalent, with almost one in five 11- to 17-year-olds reporting experiences of being maltreated by a parent or guardian during childhood (Radford *et al.*, 2011). Child maltreatment in the *family* has been the main area of concern in research, policy and practice. There is some overlap here with the theories of violence and crime discussed in Chapter 2. In contrast to theories of crime though, health and welfare professionals have paid less attention to why child maltreatment happens than to the type of person who is likely to commit abuse and the type of child who is vulnerable. Thinking about what causes child maltreatment, in the same way as thinking about what causes violent crime, is important because it influences how we respond. Often in the area of children, violence and crime, unspoken and poorly articulated assumptions about the causes of child abuse have been promoted in policy debate, campaigning and in the media. Theoretical analysis helps us to reflect on the bigger picture, to describe, analyse, critique, test and prescribe alternative ways of thinking and responding. It has relevance also to our own assumptions, beliefs and prejudices, and demands critical self-reflective scrutiny of our everyday activities as practitioners or as individuals.

In this chapter five theoretical approaches to child maltreatment will be briefly discussed:

- Attachment theory (an example of a psychological/social psychological perspective which focuses on the instinctive and psychological qualities of the individuals and on the interaction between abuser, child and immediate environment).
- Family violence and feminist perspectives (examples of sociological perspectives that emphasize social and political conditions as the most important factors explaining child abuse).
- The ecological model of child well-being (an example of an integrative approach to theory which seeks to combine individual, community and broader societal factors).
- Developmental victimology, which has expanded the theoretical horizon of child maltreatment research to include childhood victimization, the overlapping and interrelated aspects of victimization in the family, the school and the wider community.
- Childhood studies, which consider the social construction of childhood in late modernity.

Each perspective offers insights and some limitations for understanding child maltreatment. Categorization inevitably involves simplification of perspectives and readers are encouraged to follow up the further reading recommendations made at the end of this chapter to build on the knowledge gained here.

Questions considered in this chapter will be:

- How do we explain why parents/caregivers, who are expected to provide love and support for children, are also those who are most likely to abuse or neglect them when they are most vulnerable?

- What importance should be attached to individual characteristics of the child or perpetrator of abuse; the relationships and interactions between the child, others in their lives and the environment; and structural factors such as poverty, inequality or gender?
- Are our fears about and responses to child abuse part of the problem?

Attachment theory

Child protection policy and our thinking about child abuse has been greatly influenced by frequently held public enquiries into cases where children have been killed by parents or carers (Parton, 1985), the most recent being Lord Laming's review following the killing of baby Peter Connelly (Laming, 2009). There are two age peaks in homicide rates for children. The two groups most vulnerable to homicide in childhood are infants under the age of one year, who are most likely to be killed by a parent or adult living in the home, and young people in their teens, who are more likely to be killed by a peer (Finkelhor, 2007; Home Office, 2010) . The homicide rate for babies in England and Wales is the highest for all age groups in the population, being 31 homicides of under 1-year-olds per million each year, compared with 14 per million homicides for the general population (Home Office, 2010). Epidemiological studies and reviews of child abuse fatalities have confirmed the vulnerability of children in the first year of life and shown that both mothers and fathers kill children, although non-biological father figures are thought to present an increased risk (Brandon et al. 2008). Young parents living in circumstances of social deprivation, poverty, domestic violence, parental mental health, drug and alcohol problems, and males with criminal histories predominate among those who kill their children. Children with disabilities or who have had birth difficulties are also thought to face increased risk (Reder and Duncan, 1999).

The emotive response to a parent killing or starving to death their own child is often that the parent must be 'sick' or utterly 'evil'. However, looking at child abuse-related fatalities in England and Wales, Reder and Duncan observed that over 90 per cent of abusing parents are neither psychotic nor criminal personalities but instead lonely, unhappy, struggling adults living under heavy stress. According to Reder and Duncan, hitting or neglecting the child is an outcome of the interaction between the parent's functioning and the child's behaviour, their relationship together and interactions with others in their immediate world, such as partners. This is diagrammatically represented in Figure 3.1.

SOCIAL STRESS

↑

PARENTS WITH UNRESOLVED CONFLICTS

↑

VULNERABLE CHILDREN

Figure 3.1 An interactional model of child abuse
Source: Reder and Duncan (1999, p. 6)

Poor bonding between the parent and the child is relevant to a parent's unresolved conflicts and interactions with the child. Attachment theory argues that infants have an instinctive need to form a close, loving relationship with responsive people. Post-war writings on attachment were criticized for over-emphasizing the need for babies to have a bond with one caregiver, the mother, but more recent approaches suggest that an infant can bond with more than one person (Prior and Glaser, 2006). In most cases infants develop secure attachments with caregivers in early life.

An attachment is a bond between an individual, for example a baby, and an attachment figure, for example the mother. An attachment is based on the need for safety, security and protection. This is paramount in infancy and early childhood, when the developing child is immature and vulnerable. Infants instinctively attach to their carer(s). Attachment serves the specific biological function of promoting protection, survival and ultimately, genetic replication. … Attachment behaviour is **proximity seeking** to the attachment figure in the face of threat. Fear is the appreciation of danger and calls for a response, the child seeking proximity to or physical contact with the attachment figure/parent anticipating a response which will remove any threat or discomfort. The role of the attachment figure is to provide a **secure base** from which the child can explore, and **a safe haven** to which to retreat when threatened. **Separation** from the attachment figure creates **anxiety**. Attachment behaviour develops from early infancy but after age three years, it is less frequent and urgent as the maturing child feels threatened less frequently. Based on their cumulative experiences with their attachment figures, infants aged approximately 9 months have developed patterns of attachment specific to these attachment figures.

(Prior and Glaser, 2006)

Attachment has four basic characteristics:

- *Safe haven*—when the infant feels fearful, threatened or insecure, she knows she can return to the parent or carer to receive comfort and protection.
- *Secure base*—the parent or carer gives the infant a secure base from which to explore the world.
- *Proximity maintenance*—to be safe the infant strives to remain near to the parent or carer.
- *Separation distress*—When separated from the parent or carer the infant is distressed.

Theoretical developments in attachment theory came from laboratory-based observational experiments with primates and with mothers and infants. Behavioural scientists staged experiments that involved observing what happened when infants were separated from their mothers or put into 'strange situations' (Ainsworth *et al.*, 1978). The 'strange situation' research used extensively by Mary Ainsworth and colleagues is outlined in the box below.

Example of research

Strange situation experiment:

1 Parent and child are alone in the room.
2 Child explores the room without parental participation.
3 Stranger enters the room, talks to the parent, approaches the child.
4 Parent quietly leaves the room.
5 Parent then returns and comforts the child.

Ainsworth *et al.* (1978) identified three main attachment styles from their observations of mothers and infants aged between 9 and 18 months of age—secure (where the child is upset when the parent leaves but is soon comforted on return), anxious/ambivalent (where the child is greatly distressed when the parent leaves and does not appear to be comforted on return) and avoidant (where the child may avoid contact with the parent, does not seek comfort and shows little preference between the parent and stranger).

A fourth attachment pattern has since been identified, namely disorganized (Main and Solomon, 1986) where the infant displays odd behaviour, frozen stillness or no clear pattern. Most children (65%) will develop a secure attachment with a caregiver, where the child is confident the response from the caregiver will meet the need for safety and security (Prior and Glaser, 2006). The attachment process can be disrupted if:

1 The child has no consistent caregiver; for instance, if the child has been kept in an institution with minimum contact from a carer. The child can become detached and unable to give or receive affection.
2 The child's key relationships are disrupted by prolonged periods of separation, as where a parent goes in and out of prison or a child has many foster-care placements that break down. The child may feel unwanted and develop an anxious or avoidant attachment where she is uncertain of other people's love and avoids closeness for fear of further hurt or separation.
3 The child's caregiver is hostile, unresponsive or unpredictable. The child may develop an ambivalent attachment—where there is a mixture of strong positive and negative feelings—or a disorganized attachment—that lacks a clear pattern.

Children with unloving carers develop poor attachments to parents and are thought to be more likely to have difficulty in forming relationships.

Poor attachment is seen as being both a cause and consequence of child maltreatment. Howe (2005) notes that maltreating caregivers do not help their children to recognize, understand or regulate their emotions. In response, the child employs psychologically defensive strategies to keep out of consciousness the painful thought that the caregiver neither cares about nor protects them but hurts and frightens. The psychological defences are fragile and break down when the child experiences fear and threat of danger, activating the attachment system need to seek proximity, comfort and safety. Howe argues that maltreated children tend to be in one of two mental states:

• A controlling, defensive mode where the individual seeks to control or dominate all attachment-related interactions through compulsive compliance, role-reversed compulsive caregiving, compulsive self-reliance or combinations of these.
• An out-of-control helpless/hostile mode where the individual is overwhelmed by feelings of fear, danger, anger and despair as the attachment figure is perceived as dangerous and rejecting.

Child maltreatment is strongly associated with disorganized attachment. Children with this attachment pattern are more likely to show controlling behaviour as adults (Prior and Glaser, 2006), to have distorted perceptions of other people's needs and to react with hostility to perceived threats (Howe,

2005). For example, the crying baby may be perceived as deliberately trying to annoy the parent and invoke an abusive or rejecting response. While children with poor early attachments can recover in later relationships if their needs for love and stability are met, children with recurrent and prolonged attachment difficulties can have problems in adolescence and adulthood. The older the child, the more the pattern becomes resistant to change, indicating that early identification and intervention with children who have attachment problems is likely to have more positive outcomes on their overall well-being and relationships.

Reflections on the research

- How well does attachment theory explain why parents/caregivers, who are expected to provide love and support for children, are also those most likely to abuse or neglect them when they are most vulnerable?
- How well do you think the theory explains why many abused parents do not abuse their children?
- What are the implications of attachment theory for practitioners working with children and young people?
- Could the theory of attachment be applied to understanding children's aggressive and violent behaviour as discussed in Chapter 2?
- Are the causes and circumstances of the relatively rare child abuse fatalities similar to the causes and circumstances of the relatively frequent cases where children are maltreated but do not die as a result?
- What do you see to be the contributions to knowledge and limitations of this perspective?

Family violence, feminism and child abuse

Sociological perspectives on child maltreatment take a very different approach to the psychological perspectives by looking at the wider inequalities and social circumstances that give rise to child maltreatment, rather than individual behaviour. Population studies confirm that, although children from all socio-economic groups can experience maltreatment, child maltreatment is strongly associated with poverty and social deprivation (Radford *et al.*, 2011). As Corby (2006) notes, sociological perspectives on child abuse did not have much influence on child protection work in Britain before the 1990s, except in relation to sexual abuse and gender. Research from the 1970s was initially founded upon adult experiences and memories of childhood abuse and developed along two different routes—family violence research, based upon mostly quantitative, survey based research done in the USA (e.g. Straus *et al.*, 1980) and feminist research based mainly on qualitative research on adult women's experiences of lifetime abuse, including experiences in childhood (e.g. Armstrong, 1978; Hanmer and Saunders, 1985).

Example of research: the family violence perspective

The family violence perspective perceived the family as being an institution founded upon conflict, conflict between men and women and between parents and children. Family violence researchers based their thinking on findings from national surveys of adults living in the USA, the National Family Violence Surveys conducted in 1975 and 1985 (Straus *et al.*, 1980; Straus and Smith, 1990). These found high prevalence rates of physical violence in the home—violence between husbands and wives, siblings, parents towards children and children towards elders—all of which were seen to be linked. While family violence researchers acknowledge that the causes of child maltreatment and family violence are many, violence is an option available to resolve disputes where a society creates the conditions—such as family privacy—where this is acceptable. Two potent factors increase the likelihood that it will occur: social learning and stress in the context of reduced resources for coping with stress. These are likely to vary across different cultures and societies. Children learn that violence is appropriate from parents, who in many societies across the world have the state-sanctioned ability to use physical violence to 'discipline' them. However, whether or not a person will use violence depends on the level of stress and resources they have, which are affected by individual and structural factors. While stress does not cause family violence, and there are other responses to stress apart from abuse, violence is more likely in the stressful context of socially isolated low-income families. Straus and Smith (1990) maintain that, although women seldom use violence towards others outside the family, they are as likely as are men to use it against adults and children within the home. Women use more violence in the family towards children and partners because they are most likely to be exposed to the frustrations of childcare in societies where they are expected to carry the bulk of responsibility for looking after children.

Feminist researchers similarly increased awareness of previously 'hidden' forms of abuse but with greater emphasis on the institutional and everyday practices that normalize and gender experiences of violence and abuse (Stanko, 1985, 1990). Feminist thinking on child maltreatment in the 1970s is different to that which evolved after the 1990s. In the 1970s the interest was mostly in exposing patriarchal male violence towards women and challenging the 'burden' aspects of motherhood. After the 1990s, interests shifted towards diversity and differences in gendered experiences of violence, the reworking of relations of power between men and women in the politicized notion of 'shared care' for children. In contrast to family violence researchers, feminists argued that interpersonal violence in the family affects males and females very differently and there is gender asymmetry in experiences of abuse (Dobash and Dobash, 1978). Gender affects children's experiences of abuse in different ways, with older boys being the majority of victims of physical violence but girls experiencing most sexual abuse. Gender is also relevant to the study of child abuse in the family in that perpetrators of sexual abuse and domestic violence are predominantly male, while both adult males and females neglect and employ physical violence towards children in the family context.

Feminist perspectives place less emphasis on frustrations and stresses causing family violence than on power relationships that shape experiences of abuse and the political positioning of victimhood. Radical feminism explored the gendered nature of violence as rooted in patriarchy, where men assert power and control over women in the family and in everyday relationships. Looking at everyday violence and abuse in women's lives brought to the fore experiences of rape, domestic violence, child sexual abuse and powerful critiques of the role of the state, criminal justice and 'caring professions' (MacKinnon, 1989). On this perspective child abuse is an aspect of the patriarchal abuse of women by men. All forms of violence against women, and some forms of violence towards children, from the extreme (such as homicide, rape and child sexual abuse) to the everyday (domestic violence, sexual exploitation, sexual harassment and the objectification of women's bodies in pornography) are seen as linked on a continuum. Experiences are positioned on a sexual violence continuum, ranging not necessarily in terms of severity but in how we make sense of them, how they are perceived as 'normalized' or 'aberrant' (Kelly, 1988). Each experience of violence and abuse is linked to everyday, 'normal' male behaviour which oppresses and controls women. Typical and aberrant behaviour shade into one another and the boundaries between them are unclear. Experiences of violence are frequent or the fear of them happening is ever present, affecting women's, and men's, behaviour and actions, their perceptions of risk and danger, safe and unsafe places, feelings of personal responsibility and fears of crime (Hanmer and Saunders, 1985; Stanko, 1990).

Beliefs and institutional practices support patriarchal power and control over women and children. The persistence of everyday violence is supported by routine denial of men's responsibility for violence against women and children in the criminal justice system and caring professions, and the tendency to blame women for their own victimization (Edwards, 1989) and for failing to protect children (Droisen and Driver, 1989). Feminist writings about child sexual abuse and incest pre-dated the child protection 'discovery' of sexual abuse that occurred in the UK following the Cleveland inquiry in 1987 (Butler Sloss, 1988). Research critiqued the tendency in child protection, the family courts and social work to blame mothers for failing to protect children from abuse.

Up until relatively recently (the 1990s), feminist writings about children and abuse focused mainly on child sexual abuse with less attention given to physical violence and neglect or to direct research with children. By the 1990s, it was clear that the view of all interpersonal abuse in heterosexual relationships as 'male violence' towards women and children failed to consider adequately the diversity of women's, men's and children's experiences of victimization as well as women's abuse of children, partners and other adults (Kelly, 1991). Family relationships changed rapidly from the late 1970s onwards and there was a decline in experience and public policy in the post-war 'ideal' of the family as breadwinner husband and economically dependent homemaker wife responsible for all the childcare. Gendered relationships and identities have been reconfigured on the basis of men's and women's responsibilities to care for and protect children. In the late 1990s fathers' rights groups staged a series of protests (involving stunts such as men dressed up as batman dangling from cranes) targeted at 'selfish' women who squeezed men out of children's lives post-divorce. Feminist research explored the evolution of the notion of equal parental responsibility from a situation where fathers 'cared about' children, but played a minor role in providing physical care, to a situation of 'caring for' children, where physical care of the child is assumed to be, not a burden imposed by patriarchy, but more a responsibility and emotional investment held by both men and women (Radford and Hester, 2006). They critiqued the notion of ownership of the child upon which the debates about shared care rested and how the assumption that women must provide a father for a child and preserve lifelong contact between fathers and children not only ignored children's wishes and feelings but also the potential of harm to children's well-being and women's safety by continued contact with men who were perpetrators of domestic violence and child abuse (Hester *et al.*, 2007; Mullender *et al.*, 2003; Mullender and Morley, 1994 and Radford and Hester, 2006). In child protection and family law, violent fathers are absent as are children's voices and, the focus of work on mothers, places all responsibility on women to make children safe, while denying the impact that trauma and living with abuse has on their ability to do so (Hooper, 2010; Radford and Hester, 2006).

Reflections on the theory and the research

- How well do feminist perspectives explain why parents/caregivers, who are expected to provide love and support for children, are also those most likely to abuse or neglect them when they are most vulnerable?
- What does taking a gendered approach to violence mean for understanding children's and young people's vulnerabilities to experience violence or abuse at different developmental ages?
- How well do you think these approaches explain why some men and boys are not violent and why some girls and women use violence in the family and close personal relationships?
- What are the implications of taking a feminist perspective for working with children living with domestic violence and working with parents of pre-schoolchildren?
- What do you see to be the contributions to and limitations of this perspective?
- What are the implications of feminist perspectives for practitioners working with children and young people living with violence?

The ecological perspective

Integrated approaches to theory are based on the premise that there is no single factor that can provide a satisfactory explanation as to why child maltreatment happens. Integrated perspectives therefore combine individual, family, environmental and societal/structural perspectives and look at the causal interactions that occur at all levels. In recent years, the public health approach to violence prevention, promoted by organizations such as WHO (see Krug et al., 2002) and the Atlanta-based Centers for Disease Control and Prevention in the USA (see www.cdc.org) has been influential in guiding understanding and interventions to prevent child maltreatment. The WHO public health perspective applies an epidemiological (disease control) approach to the study of the prevention of child maltreatment and violence in communities, defining and scoping the scale of the problem, researching key risks and protective factors, and using research to evaluate interventions experimentally (Butchart et al., 2006).

The origins of the ecological perspective on child maltreatment (reflected in the framework of assessment in child welfare practice in England discussed in Chapter 7) are mostly attributed to the work of Bronfenbrenner (1977, 1986). Writing from a child development perspective, Bronfenbrenner shifted attention from just focusing on parental stress and observations of a child's interaction with the mother by proposing a nested model of spheres of influence to represent the developing child's interaction with their family, community and wider environment.

The ecological perspective has since been widely used in research on child maltreatment (see e.g. Belsky, 1980; Freisthler *et al.*, 2006), intimate partner violence (Hagemann-White, 2010) and youth violence (Krug *et al.*, 2002). WHO's approach to the ecological perspective, a practical and simplified version of Bronfenbrenner's original model, is illustrated in Figure 3.2.

Developmental outcomes are directly influenced by the child's interactions at the four levels illustrated in the model and their 'progressive accommodation' or adaptation to these aspects of the wider environment influencing everyday life.

At the **individual level** (sometimes referred to as the ontogenetic level) are the individual characteristics of the child, including inherited genetic and biological factors, the child's age, disability or health, and the individual characteristics of the child's parents, which can influence susceptibility to maltreatment.

The **relationship level** refers to the child's or young person's interactions with others in the context of close relationships (family, friends, peers and intimate partners), which can influence vulnerability to maltreatment and victimization, as well as the likelihood of perpetrating abuse against others.

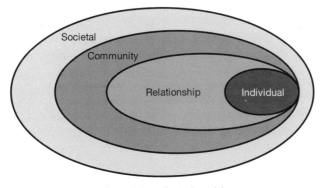

Figure 3.2 Ecological model
Source: Adapted from Krug *et al.* (2002, p. 12)

The **community level** incorporates the settings and institutions in which the child's relationships and interactions take place (the neighbourhood, schools, residential units, workplaces and criminal justice agencies), which can contribute to child maltreatment.

Finally, at the **societal level,** there are the laws, cultural and belief systems, social inequalities and political issues, such as gender inequality, social exclusion and poverty, and failure to challenge physical punishment of children, which can provide environments that allow maltreatment to thrive.

The child's vulnerabilities within the ecological approach are not fixed and may change over the life course with the child's developmental process. Bronfenbrenner referred to this process of change over time as the 'chrono-system' (Bronfenbrenner, 1986). A number of factors at each level are associated with increased risk that a child or young person will be maltreated, and for some children, risks may accumulate with age (Bentovim *et al.*, 2009). There are also some factors that work protectively to prevent or mitigate adverse impact upon a particular child. A summary of some of these risk factors, based upon WHO and other child protection publications (Bentovim *et al.*, 2009; Butchart *et al.*, 2006; Krug *et al.*, 2002; Newman, 2004) is presented in Table 3.1.

Table 3.1 also includes some of the factors that are known or thought to work protectively, although as yet far less is known from research about some of these factors, especially at the societal level, where cross-national comparative research is needed. While the presence of any one risk factor is unlikely to result in maltreatment, the existence of two or more, particularly in the absence of protective supports, will substantially increase the chances of it occurring.

It is beyond the scope of this chapter to describe all the different ways in which risk and protective factors might work together to influence child maltreatment, a good overview may be found in Belsky (1993) and in Bentovim *et al.* (2009). Nevertheless, it is important to note that these factors are not necessarily causal and are likely to interact in complex ways. For example, childhood hobbies may work to protect children from abuse, but are also likely to be related to a warm and supportive parental environment that may, in turn, be reciprocally associated with the child's intelligence and disposition.

The public health approach has helped to guide researchers, practitioners and policy-makers towards identifying factors and interventions that may reduce and prevent child maltreatment. This approach to thinking about

Table 3.1 Common risk and protective factors for child maltreatment

Ecological level	Risk factors	Protective factors
Individual	Age of the child High needs as a result of premature birth, low birth weight, disability Serious illness Temperament: persistent crying Prior victimization Feelings of insecurity; low self-esteem Depression/anxiety	Good health and development Above-average intelligence Hobbies and interests Personality factors Easy temperament Positive disposition Active coping style Positive self-esteem Good social skills
Relationships and Family	Domestic violence Parent with poor impulse control Parent with past history of child maltreatment Large family size Household overcrowding Single parenthood Poor parenting as a result of parent's young age or poor education Social isolation, lack of social support Parental psychopathology Substance abuse Separation/divorce, especially high-conflict divorce High stress Difficulties in bonding/attachment Parent's or young person's antisocial behaviour or criminal activity Parent's use of physical punishment	Secure attachment to adult family member Warm parent–child relationship, high level of care during childhood Supportive family environment Extended family support and involvement, including childcare Good peer relationships Lack of abuse-related stress
Community	Low socio-economic status Lack of access to social support, including child and social care services Unemployment Low social capital Dangerous/violent neighbourhood, tolerance of violence in neighbourhood Easily available alcohol	Access to healthcare, therapeutic and social services Supportive adults outside of family Social cohesion in community
Societal	Cultural values and beliefs Gender inequalities Child and family policies Lack of preventive healthcare Lack of required protection from violence Existence of child pornography, child labour or sexual exploitation War or social conflict	Enforcement and legal protection from violence and maltreatment Gender equality measures Implementation of children's rights

child maltreatment has been helpful to challenge stereotypes, focus on the individual child in context, and to consider not only the challenges in protecting children from harm but also the potential to strengthen resilience and build support. As such it has been popular within social work where it is the preferred option to build a supportive alliance with parents in order to protect a child, rather than to 'police' families.

However, although the ecological model has been promoted as an 'integrated' approach to theorizing violence, psychological, behavioural and interactional factors of child abuse have tended to dominate the research literature. Violence tends to be de-gendered and depoliticized and policy responses are sometimes reduced to managing a checklist of individualized risks and protective factors.

Reflections on the theory and research

- How well do you think the ecological perspective explains why some people are violent and others are not?
- How well do you think the ecological perspective explains violence and sexual abuse towards children perpetrated by peers?
- What importance should be attached to individual characteristics of the child or perpetrator of abuse; the relationships and interactions between the child, others in their lives and the environment; and structural factors such as poverty, inequality or gender?
- What are the implications for practice of taking an ecological perspective to understand child maltreatment? Consider this question with reference to children living with domestic violence.
- What do you consider to be the contributions and limitations of this perspective?

Developmental victimology

As in theories of crime and violence (Chapter 2) researchers on child maltreatment have recently investigated how children's experiences of violence and abuse vary developmentally. David Finkelhor's work over many years has contributed significantly to knowledge in this area (Finkelhor 2007). Finkelhor's work has developed from his involvement with family violence researchers, particularly Murray Straus, at the University of New Hampshire in the USA and the basic tenets of the family violence researchers and the emphasis upon empirical, largely quantitative survey-based research are a fundamental part and development of this approach. Developmental victimology has expanded the horizons of child maltreatment research in three ways:

- In the definition and categorization of child victimization;
- By focusing on children's and young people's experiences of victimization;
- Considering how victimization changes across the course of childhood.

For maltreatment research, the focus on victimization challenges the adult-led categorization of different experiences of child abuse and maltreatment into those that matter and those that do not. Victimization is different from other forms of trauma and adversity, like bereavement or natural disasters, because there is usually another person involved as a perpetrator, there is often motivation and intent, and the victimization raises issues such as abuse of trust, betrayal, injustice or immorality. Methodologically and conceptually, victimization covers all forms of interpersonal victimization experienced in childhood—robbery; physical violence; sibling violence; bullying; sexual harassment; exposure to domestic violence; sexual abuse; child abuse and neglect; community violence; physical punishment; and abuse in young people's intimate relationships. Victimization covers three categories: (1) *conventional crimes* in which children are victims (e.g. rape, robbery, assault, kidnap); (2) *child maltreatment* acts that violate child welfare statutes such as abuse or neglect by a parent or caregiver; (3) *non-crimes* acts that would be crimes if the victims were adults (e.g. peer-to-peer abuse in schools). There is some overlap between these categories (Figure 3.3).

Victimization includes a wide range of criminal behaviour as well as behaviour that is neither recognized as being criminal nor is a matter for child protection services, even though it causes or has potential to cause harm to children (e.g. bullying by peers). Some forms of victimization such as sibling violence or physical punishment by a parent, although harmful, are normalized.

Child victimization differs from adult victimization because it raises dependency issues. Finklehor argues that experiences of victimization can be arranged on a continuum of dependency status, ranging from high dependency-related victimization through to non-dependency-related victimization. Child neglect would sit at the high end of the dependency continuum because it is a form of victimization that happens mostly to children (and occasionally to adults who are ill, disabled or elderly) who depend on an adult for their daily care. Child abduction in the family and emotional abuse

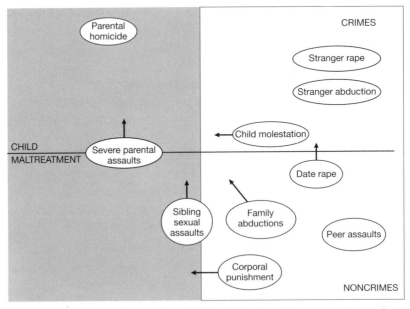

Figure 3.3 Conceptual geography of child victimization: Crimes, non-crimes and child maltreatment
Source: Finkelhor (2008, p. 25)

are also strongly linked with children's developmental relationships with caregivers and sit at the high end of the dependency continuum. Physical violence, homicide and stranger abductions sit at the non-dependency end of the continuum and are victimizations that occur also to adults. Sexual abuse sits in the middle between dependency and non-dependency related, as children are likely to be sexually abused and exploited both by adults in positions of trust and by peers.

Reflections on the theory

Compare and contrast Liz Kelly's sexual violence continuum with Finkelhor's dependency continuum. What are the similarities and differences?

For Finkelhor, it is unhelpful to consider victimization experiences in isolation, to consider only parental neglect, for instance, because victimization experiences tend to accumulate, overlap and are interrelated. Some children experience 'polyvictimization', i.e. abuse from a range of different perpetrators with compounding impact. Victimization is a condition or a process and not just an event. The consequences of child maltreatment cannot be fully understood or addressed unless it is studied in the context of the range of children's experiences of victimization.

For child protection work it is important to recognize that the types of victimization experienced and the perpetrators responsible change over childhood. Early victimization experiences tend to be associated with younger children's dependency and the settings in which they live. Thus younger children are more likely to be victimized at home and less likely to be victimized by strangers or in the community. Older children are exposed to a wider range of perpetrators because they have a wider range of relationships and spend more time outside the family home. Gender is relevant to developmental experiences of victimization in childhood, in the home, school and community. Finkelhor argues that victimizations are less gender specific for younger children; boys and girls are similarly at risk of abuse and neglect in the family. However, as the child grows older, more gendered, adult patterns of victimization emerge with teenage boys suffering more overall victimizations than girls but girls experiencing much more sexual abuse.

Reflections on the theory and the research

- How well do you think developmental victimology explains why some people are violent and others are not?
- What do you see to be the contributions and limitations of this perspective?
- What are the implications of developmental victimology for policy and practice? Consider this with reference to young people's experiences of violence in their own intimate partner relationships.

Childhood studies

The growing concern about child abuse

The phenomenon of child abuse has emerged as a malign and exponential growth towards the conclusion of the twentieth century not because of any significant

⇨

The growing concern about child abuse—Cont'd

alteration in the pattern of our behaviour towards children but because of the changing patterns of personal, political and moral control in social life more generally which have, in turn, affected our vision of childhood. Whereas an antique vision of the child rendered abuse unseen or unintelligible, modernity illuminated mistreatment and highlighted the necessity of care. However, the late-modern, emergent vision of the child ... brings abuse into prominence through scrutiny and surveillance but also through the peculiar structural demands on the constitution of personal identity and social relationships wrought through accelerative social change.

Jenks, 1996, p. 86.

Childhood studies writers such as Jenks placed childhood itself and child abuse in the spotlight by looking at the social construction of childhood in late modernity. Children in late modernity appear as idealized types, as innocent victims or hedonistic villains, contributing to adult feelings of security and insecurity. In the unspecified status of the developing child, the child as 'becoming', childhood sequesters adult experience, has grown in duration, demands more adult labour, affective and emotional investment. From this perspective child abuse has not grown in prevalence but it has grown in significance so that we are obsessed with the risks to children and the risks they pose to others. A powerful discourse of victimhood has emerged, as may be seen in high street bookshops where whole sections are now set aside for autobiographical texts on traumatic life stories. Both media and child protection charities have a tendency to portray children as passive victims of adult abuse, denying them any agency, their individual efforts to resist, the informal support which children give other children and reinforcing their dependence on adults (Kitzinger, 1997). The increased worries about children have brought unprecedented surveillance, regulation and monitoring of children's lives to protect them from harm, and to identify and spot early on those likely to develop into troublesome children and dangerous adults.

In earlier chapters we have looked at public concerns about risks to children, how these constrain and structure children's lives so that children are more supervised by adults, spend most of their time indoors and have less time or places in which to play (Guldberg, 2009).

Are our fears about and responses to child abuse part of the problem?

Nigel Parton has written extensively over many years about child maltreatment theory and policy (Parton, 1985, 1997, 2006; Frost amd Parton, 2009), looking at the periodical surges in public concern which gave rise to enquiries such as the Laming enquiry into the murder of Victoria Climbié (Laming, 2003), or the Soham murders of Holly Jackson and Jessica Payne in 2005. These enquiries have forensically examined 'failures' to protect children who were killed by abusive adults. Parton considers historically how policy, practice, social movements (such as the NSPCC and feminism) and the media have socially constructed the problem of child abuse and who is 'dangerous', contributing to these periodic moral panics. The preoccupation with risk has affected everyone, but its impact is unequal.

Child abuse in late modernity is an expanded but contested concept, leading to uncertainty about what it is and to the fear of failing to spot it. This demands a more complex, information sharing, multi-agency/partnership response, which because of its complexity presents further risk of getting things wrong. As concepts of child abuse expand—to recognize problems such as emotional abuse, for example—the challenges of child protection increase, more families come into the net of child protection responsibility, at the same time in which responsibilities to deal with this are dispersed and more diversely shared between state and civil society.

Like feminists, writers in the area of new childhood studies are interested in adult emotional responses to and investments in children and child abuse. It is not just the case that our obsession with risk has gone too far and exaggerated risks to children, as suggested by some (Furedi and Bristow, 2008; Guldberg, 2009). A great deal of child abuse still happens in the family and in the context of supposedly intimate and 'caring' relationships. However, emotional responses to child abuse, anger and disgust at how people can do these things to children, are projected, as seen in media representations, on to lurking paedophiles, who present a danger to all children, or collusive, feckless and generally irresponsible single mothers. Concern about (largely media-driven) risks impacts upon the need to identify, manage, reduce and avert risks in parental and state responses, contributing to increased parental monitoring of children and an exhausting proliferation of policies and procedures to identify, reduce and avert risk in children's social care. The paedophile needs identifying and risk management, and the abusive, hard-to-reach, socially excluded family needs targeting, early intervention and prevention. The 'public health approach' to child abuse prevention, which is generally viewed as being benign, is part of a net widening process of the increased surveillance of child welfare. Child protection has consequently developed into a system characterized by target-driven bureaucratic monitoring and surveillance of populations, particularly of socially excluded communities, to assess 'progress'.

Childhood studies perspectives challenge thinking about children being no more than a developmental bundle of needs or uncontrolled urges to be moulded by adult guidance. They problematize adults' relationships with children and the role rising concerns about child abuse play in the regulation and supervision of children. It could be argued that neither Parton nor Jenks draw much from children's own perspectives and views about abuse, children studied as beings in their own right, as agents who influence, as well as being shaped by the world in which they live.

Reflections on the theory and the research

- How well do you think childhood studies approaches explain why some people are violent and others are not?
- What are the implications of childhood studies for policy and practice? Consider this with reference to children living with domestic violence.
- What new research questions might this approach pose for the study of child maltreatment?
- What do you see to be the contributions and limitations of this perspective?

Summary

- Single-factor explanations of the causes of child maltreatment cannot explain adequately why some children and young people experience abuse and victimization while others do not, although psychological and socio-psychological research such as research on attachment has practical value in its potential to support loving and secure relationships between parents and children.
- Integrative theories have helped us to understand the complexity of individual children's experiences of maltreatment and these can provide a useful framework for assessment of the child's needs, vulnerabilities and protective factors in the network of social relationships. Ending child abuse however will require more than tackling a list of individual and environmental risks.
- Structural factors, such as the status of children, poverty, inequality and gender, create conditions in which maltreatment flourishes. Awareness of these factors is highly relevant to intervention and professional practice.
- Child maltreatment is not a historically new invention but our efforts to control it can contribute to the problem.

Further reading

Finkelhor, D. (2007) *Childhood Victimization*. Oxford: Oxford University Press.

This book brings together several years of research on child victimization and provides a clear explanation of the developmental victimology approach.

Hooper, C. (2010) 'Gender, child maltreatment and young people's offending', in Featherstone, B., Hooper, C., Scourfiels, J. and Taylor, J. (eds) *Gender and Child Welfare in Society*. Chichester: Wiley.

Hooper reviews the gendered aspects in the impact of child maltreatment.

Jenks, C. (1996) *Childhood* London: Routledge.

One of the earlier texts in the field of new childhood studies which historically reviews the social construction of childhood.

Parton, N. (2006) *Safeguarding Childhood*. Basingstoke: Palgrave.

A thorough, critical analysis of policy on child protection and safeguarding, risk and the growth of surveillance of children and parents.

Prior, V. and Glaser, D. (2006) *Understanding Attachment and Attachment Disorders: Theory Evidence and Practice*. London: JKP.

A theoretical review and research-based exploration of attachment, its impact on development and of professional interventions with those affected by attachment disorders.

Research details

Attachment—Mary Ainsworth

Researchers observed children aged 12 to 18 months as they responded to situations where they were briefly left alone and then reunited with their mothers.

Ainsworth, M., Blehar, M., Waters, E. and Wall, S. (1978) *Patterns of Attachment*. Hillsdale, NJ: Erlbaum.

Family violence perspective—Straus, Gelles and Steinmetz

Straus, Gelles and Steinmetz carried out two national surveys of violence in the family in the USA in 1976 and 1986. In 1976 they interviewed a nationally representative sample of 2,145 adult family members. In 1986 they telephone interviewed a nationally representative sample of 6,002 family members. The Conflict Tactics Scale was the measure of violence used in the research.

Gelles, R. and Straus, M. (1988) *Intimate Violence*. New York: Simon & Schuster.

Straus, M., Gelles, R. and Steinmetz, S. (1980) *Behind Closed Doors: Violence in the American Family*. New York: Anchor Press.

Part 3
Implications for Children's Lives

Consequences 4

Introduction and key questions

Globally, violence has a very significant impact on children's health, well-being and life chances. However, as previously argued, the impact on individual children is not the same, even in the same family. A range of protective factors and vulnerabilities at the individual, family, community and societal level interact to influence experiences of growing up in contemporary Britain.

The research into the consequences of living with violence and abuse shares some of the difficulties that exist on research into prevalence (as discussed in Chapter 1). Studies have often been based on clinical or convenience samples rather than on samples of participants drawn from and representative of the general population. Definitions and measures of maltreatment and impact have varied. When looking at outcomes in later life it can be difficult to distinguish the impact of violence and maltreatment from the consequences of living with other adversities, such as poverty, homelessness, bereavement and family separation, that are often associated with growing up with violence or abuse. Some of these methodological challenges can be addressed by conducting prospective, longitudinal studies, which track cohorts of children from birth over a number of years to consider outcomes. However, these are rare and very costly.

The research on impact varies in the approach taken to gather evidence. Epidemiological and clinical researchers focus on large samples and quantitative analysis and experiences become statistics. Qualitative research, often conducted by sociologists, has been mostly based on adults' reflections on their childhood experiences. Research done directly with children and young people themselves is relatively recent. Not knowing how to ask, which methods of research with children are appropriate and how to deal with the ethical issues has, until recently, been a barrier to development (see Chapter 1). As a result the research literature is skewed towards the clinical and filtered by adult concerns and interests.

Questions considered in this chapter will be:

- What does research reveal about the short-term and longer term consequences of child maltreatment?
- What does research reveal about whether some children are more vulnerable and others apparently more resilient to longer term adverse consequences?

The impact on health and behaviour

What does research reveal about the short-term and longer term consequences of child maltreatment?

The WHO global report on violence helpfully summarized the consequences that child maltreatment can have for children (Krug *et al.*, 2002). An adapted version of the summary is presented in Table 4.1. Some of the consequences are lifelong and life-threatening.

Immediate consequences

The World Health Organization has estimated that 155,000 child deaths in children under 15 occur worldwide each year as a result of abuse or neglect, which is 0.6 per cent of all deaths and 12.7 per cent of deaths due to an injury. Only one-third of these deaths are classified as homicide

Table 4.1 Health consequences of child maltreatment

Physical	Death
	Abdominal/thoracic injuries
	Brain injuries
	Chronic pain
	Impact on brain development
	Bruises and welts
	Burns and scalds
	Central nervous system injuries
	Disability
	Fractures
	Lacerations and abrasions
	Ocular damage
	Cancer
	Chronic lung disease
	Fibromyalgia
	Irritable bowel syndrome
	Ischaemic heart disease
	Liver disease
Sexual and reproductive	Reproductive health problems
	Sexual dysfunction
	Sexually transmitted diseases, including HIV/AIDS
	Unwanted pregnancy
Psychological and behavioural	Alcohol and drug abuse
	Cognitive impairment
	Delinquent, violent and other risk-taking behaviours
	Conduct disorders
	Depression and anxiety
	Developmental delays
	Eating and sleep disorders
	Feelings of shame and guilt
	Hyperactivity
	Poor relationships and attachment problems
	Poor school performance
	Poor self-esteem
	Post-traumatic stress disorder
	Psychosomatic disorders
	Suicidal behaviour and self-harm

(Gilbert *et al.*, 2008a). Child maltreatment-related deaths are relatively rare events in the UK; however, infants aged under 12 months have the greatest risk. The most frequent cause of death are injuries to the head or internal organs. Other causes are intentional suffocation, shaking and, more rarely, choking or battering (Pinheiro, 2006). Obtaining evidence of non-accidental injury or child neglect to support a criminal prosecution can be difficult and there has been controversy and criticism of expert medical evidence. The majority of murders of children aged under 1 are perpetrated by one or both parents, mothers and fathers being likely to kill an infant (Home Office, 2010).

The immediate consequences of maltreatment, apart from fatality, include physical injuries, cognitive impairment, failure to thrive, and the psychological and emotional consequences of experiencing and witnessing abuse—fear, confusion, anger, feelings of rejection, anxiety, trauma and low self-esteem (Corby, 2006).

Psychological and emotional impact

A large number of research studies show that it is the emotional and psychological impact of violence and abuse that most often debilitates and disadvantages individuals (see Corby (2006) for further discussion). The nature of the relationship between perpetrator and victim influences the emotional and psychological impact. In the context of a close relationship, an abuser has ready, constant access to the victim and expert knowledge on how best to cause hurt or upset. There is often an age- or gender-related imbalance of power or a dependency relationship between the victim and abuser. Family relationships are expected to be nurturing relationships based on love, so the potential for abusers in the family to cause psychological or emotional harm, or to betray trust, is greatest (Browne and Finkelhor, 1985).

The psychological and emotional impact of sexual abuse can be particularly devastating because the secrecy and stigma surrounding child sexual abuse means that children who experience this often have to cope alone. Abuse or neglect by a caregiver is likely to affect the child's attachment to that parent. The victim's strong emotional ties can draw them to defend family members, even when the family is highly abusive and the loyalty and affection are not reciprocated (Mudaly and Goddard, 2006). There is often an unwritten code of family privacy that makes it more difficult to get help, to be believed and to have complaints taken seriously. Developmental and social factors make it difficult for children to recognize and talk about experiences of violence and abuse. This may be particularly so for abuse in the family or in close relationships that start early on in a child's life because, until the child is able to extend social networks and relationships outside the family or close relationship, what is experienced may be understood to be 'what happens'.

Example of research—young people's views on maltreatment

Mudaly and Goddard (2006) found that some of the children whom they interviewed about experiences of abuse had thought what was happening to them was 'normal' at the time, and it was not until they were older and had wider interactions with people outside the immediate family that they started to question this.

> 'Things were very normal for me. I saw things as being very normal. I didn't know any differently. I mean I wasn't ecstatic with life but there weren't any disruptions, I was just going along with it. ... It was just like washing the dishes or taking the dog for a walk. The abuse just slotted into it all.'
>
> (18-year-old female talking about childhood sexual abuse in Mudaly and Goddard, 2006, p. 80)

Question

What are the implications of this for public education about violence and maltreatment in childhood?

Younger children may be aware of problems but may be less likely than older children to understand what is happening and why.

> 'I didn't quite understand it when I was so young, because ... I just got used to it, when he used to hit me and my little brother and then my mum. I just got used to it.'
>
> (Marilyn, aged 15, McGee, 2000, p. 98)

There are also barriers to talking about the abuse or violence that will prevent it from coming to light.

Case study

Rachel is 13 years old and lives with her mother Susan, father Brian and younger sister Laura, aged 4. Brian is a controlling and violent man who abuses his partner, and uses physical punishment and harsh rigid discipline towards his daughters. Rachel has also been sexually abused by her father since the age of 3. Rachel is getting into trouble at school because of aggressive behaviour towards other pupils. She is mixing with a group of young people who hang around the local park and streets smoking and drinking alcohol. She has been cutting her legs on a regular basis with a Stanley knife.

Activity

Make a list of the possible reasons why Rachel might find it difficult to tell an adult about the sexual abuse she is experiencing.

Reasons why a child or young person may not disclose experiences of living with maltreatment

These include:

- Not recognizing the behaviour as abuse.
- Fear of the consequences.
- Thinking they are to blame for the abuse.
- Feeling ashamed.
- Attachment to the abuser.
- Being 'groomed' or frightened by the abuser into silence (Howe, 2005).
- Children may give non-verbal signals indicating that they are being harmed—having tantrums, running away, avoidance (Alaggia, 2004).
- Adults may also fail to hear or act on what a young person says or fail to recognize non-verbal indicators from the child that there is something wrong (Alaggia, 2004).

Awareness of the possible indicators and non-verbal signs is important if adults are to offer a timely response.

If the abuse is discovered, and this is particularly so for sexual abuse, the perpetrator often denies that it happened, downplays its harmfulness or argues that the child was a 'willing' participant (Finkelhor, 2008). Since disclosure is recognized as being a process (Alaggio, 2004) victims may also retract and deny what they previously said. In these circumstances the quality of the relationship with the person told initially about the violence or abuse has an important influence on whether the child or young person is later able to feel safe enough to talk again about what is happening to them (Cossar *et al.*, 2011).

The child–perpetrator relationship, it has been argued, sets the stage for a child's belief about themselves and their learning to relate to others throughout their lives.

Traumagenic dynamics of sexual abuse

Browne and Finkelhor (1985) argued that four traumagenic dynamics are at the core of the psychological injury of child sexual abuse.

1 *Traumatic sexualization*—refers to the process in which the child's sexuality (feelings and attitudes) is shaped in a developmentally inappropriate way as ⇨

---

a result of the sexual abuse. The child may, for example, develop sexually inappropriate behaviour or learn to manipulate sexually for gifts or affection.

2 *Betrayal*—refers to the process of the child discovering the person whom they depend on will harm or not protect them. The child may as a result lack trust in others and have difficulties in relationships.

3 *Powerlessness*—refers to the process where the child is made to feel unable to escape or do anything to stop the abuse. This can distort the child's sense of ability to control her life.

4 *Stigmatization*—refers to the shame, guilt and feelings of being bad communicated to the child so that his sense of value or worth is distorted.

These four traumagenic dynamics associated with the abuse distort the child's self-concept, worldview and affective capacities. Subsequent events can further impact upon the four dynamics. Two factors exert a particularly strong influence:

1 The family's reaction to the child's disclosure of the abuse—disbelief, shame and blame will add to the traumagenic impact.

2 The social and institutional response to the child's disclosure—the child may be ostracized, treated as 'damaged goods' by peers, humiliated and frightened in court.

(Browne and Finkelhor, 1985)

All these factors make maltreatment and victimization within the family or in a close relationship particularly harmful for children and young people.

The mental health consequences, illustrated in Rachel's case study above, can include low self-esteem and depression, post-traumatic stress, self-harm, suicidal ideation and suicide, drug and alcohol abuse, and eating disorders. If, as is often the case in sexual abuse, the abuser couches the behaviour in terms of an act of love, it is not surprising that a child will feel confused and self-blaming.

- Research in the UK found a statistically significant association between children's experiences of child maltreatment and suicidal intent and self-harming behaviour.
- Children and young people aged 11 to 17 who had been severely maltreated by a parent or guardian were over six times (6.4) more likely to have current suicidal ideation than non-severely maltreated children.
- They were almost four times (3.9) more likely to have self-harming thoughts (Radford *et al.*, 2011).

⇨

- One-quarter of maltreated children meet the criteria for depression in their late twenties and they have double the risk of suicide in early adulthood (Gilbert *et al.*, 2008a).
- Post-traumatic stress disorder (PTSD) and its associated features of experiencing flashbacks, hypervigilance, numbing, sleeplessness and a preoccupation with the traumatic event may be experienced by children.
- Neglected and abused children are more likely to be hyperactive, develop antisocial behaviour and engage in delinquency, substance abuse and risky sexual behaviour (Lazenbatt, 2010).
- Abused and neglected children may be aggressive with peers, be more withdrawn and have difficulty forming friendships.

Activity

The research findings on the impact of maltreatment upon children's mental health and emotional well-being demonstrate the importance of providing a timely response to children who are troubled as a result of having been abused.

What sources of emotional and psychological support and advice are available for Rachel in the area in which you live? Would a timely response be possible?

What does research reveal about whether some children are more vulnerable and others apparently more resilient to longer term adverse consequences?

Corby (2006) reviews research which suggests that the earlier the onset of the maltreatment and the longer it persists, the less likely it is that the child will be popular with peers. They might stick out as different to peers, being poorly dressed, having poor personal hygiene, lacking confidence and the opportunities which non-maltreated children have to socialize, bring friends home and take part in out-of-school activities. Maltreated children are more likely to underachieve at school. Research that has compared the performance of maltreated children with the educational performance of non-maltreated children has found significantly poorer grades in maltreated children (Kendall-Tackett, 1996; Kurtz *et al.*, 1993). Prospective studies measuring outcomes for children and young people longitudinally have found that maltreated children are more likely to have poorer educational attainment, increased special educational needs and problems with school attendance (Gilbert *et al.*, 2008a).

Children who live with abuse and violence at home may be more likely to run away, drift into street life and are vulnerable to sexual exploitation (Rees, 1993). Research suggests that sexual victimization experiences can put the victim at further risk in two ways—the trauma consequences may increase the victim's contact with perpetrators (for example, the young person may turn to substances to cope and then be at risk abuse); and perpetrators may be able to identify the young person's vulnerabilities and target them (Newman, 2004). There is little evidence however that the victim's personality factors influence the likelihood of revictimization. Vulnerability and situational factors seem to have greater impact (Macy, 2007).

The impact of abuse is compounded if the child or young person experiences multiple types of victimization, what is called 'polyvictimization', so that the child who is abused and neglected at home also experiences violence and abuse from other adults and peers at school and in the community.

Example of research—polyvictimization

Children who experience child maltreatment, sexual abuse or physical violence are at greater risk of re-victimization (Finkelhor *et al.*, 2005a) and polyvictimization (Finkelhor *et al.*, 2005b), with the risks of victimization and trauma impact increasing with age (Finkelhor *et al.*, 2009). Exploring data from a national study in the USA of children's experiences of victimization (the Developmental Victimization Survey (DVS)) Finkelhor, Ormrod, Turner and Hamby found that children with four or more different experiences of victimization in the past year, children who were 'polyvictims', were more likely than were children who had experienced one type of victimization to have high trauma symptoms. While certain types of victimization are thought generally to be more severe or more likely to be traumatizing (e.g. being injured, maltreated by a caregiver, sexually abused, attacked with a weapon), the researchers found that children who were polyvictims had higher trauma symptoms than even those children who repeatedly experienced a single form of victimization. To tackle the adverse consequences it is important that professionals who work with children and young people explore beyond presenting issues to look holistically at all experiences of violence and abuse and how these interact.

Interview with Sherry Hamby about her research

Professor Sherry Hamby, Editor of the journal *Psychology of Violence* and Research Associate Professor of Psychology at Sewanee, the University of the South, USA.

Lorraine Radford: What do you think are the most important aspects of polyvictimization for practitioners to know about when working with children and young people at different developmental stages?

⇨

Interview with Sherry Hamby about her research—Cont'd

Sherry Hamby: There are three key findings that I think are critically important for practitioners to know. First, although we are all used to referring to children as 'abused' or 'bullied' or 'molested', in fact there really are not separate populations of children who have only experienced one type of abuse or victimization. For the most part, whether we recognize it or not, we are all focusing on highly overlapping groups of children who are vulnerable in multiple settings.

Second, polyvictimization, which really captures both the number of different ways that a youth has been victimized and the number of dangerous environments to which a youth has been exposed, is more important than any particular single type of victimization. Polyvictimization is 'king of the jungle' when it comes to predicting mental health outcomes—polyvictimization has a stronger association with mental health symptoms than any single type of victimization. This is true even in comparison to the most severe victimizations such as sexual victimizations and those perpetrated by caregivers. Focusing on safety in one setting—such as addressing bullying in school—is not likely to help a child's mental health if they are also being victimized at home and in their neighbourhoods.

Finally, it is important to know that there are developmental changes in polyvictimization across the span of childhood. First, even very young infants and toddlers can be polyvictims, but it takes fewer incidents to put them in the highest risk category for their age group. They are also more likely to be victimized by siblings than older children. Problems with bullying peak in middle childhood (10- to 13-year-olds) and then drop during later adolescence. In contrast, sexual victimizations and witnessing community violence increase steadily and peak in later adolescence. None the less, whatever form it takes, polyvictimization is strongly associated with distress at all developmental stages.

Lorraine Radford: What does the research tell us about gender and victimization? Are there any gender differences in young people's experiences of polyvictimization?

Sherry Hamby: There are substantial gender differences in youth victimization. The largest gender differences are for sexual victimization, which is experienced by substantially more females than males. Most sexual victimizations involve male perpetrators and female victims, although female-on-male and male-on-male offences are not rare.

Physical victimizations show a different pattern; there are more male victims for most forms of physical assault, with male-on-male assaults being the most common pattern. There are fewer

⇨

gender differences for child maltreatment, probably because many families have both male and female children who are being maltreated. Property crimes and witnessing violence also show few gender differences, which makes sense because often the perpetrator may not even be aware of the gender of the theft victim or witness. Because there are some categories of victimization that show few gender differences, poly-victimization also is about equally common for both males and females across the span of childhood.

Longer term consequences

In the longer term childhood experiences of violence or maltreatment can affect health in adulthood. Childhood experiences of maltreatment and violence have been linked to alcohol and drug abuse, cancer, chronic lung disease, depression, obesity, liver disease and sexual and reproductive health problems, and unwanted pregnancy (Butchart *et al.*, 2006; Pinheiro, 2006). The harmful health effects are thought to be partly due to an association between child maltreatment and risk-taking behaviour which has consequences for health. Research shows that risk taking is more common among maltreated children and young people and among those who are life course persistent offenders (Piquero *et al.*, 2007). Some harmful behaviours such as smoking, binge drinking, drug taking, overeating may be coping behaviours which are particularly evident in adolescence.

Example of research—children with child protection plans

Research with 26 children and young people with child protection plans but mostly still living at home found that having friends to confide in was an important part of coping (Cossar *et al.*, 2011). Coping also included behaviour that helped young people feel better but was likely to be harmful—fighting back against bullies, missing school, shutting down, taking drugs, getting drunk or self-harming.

'A couple of weeks ago I cut myself, but you could see where I was doing it I wasn't doing it to kill myself I was doing it to like, because my friend was like threatening to hit me and that, so to take the pain away from losing my friends I had to do something to hurt myself.'

(Carol, aged 14, Cossar *et al.*, 2011)

Research that has directly asked children and young people about self-harm and risky behaviour has shed a different light on understanding the rationale and how it relates to coping. Children and young people may need help to find alternative, less harmful strategies for coping with experiences of violence and abuse.

Developmental Dimensions Model of Victimization Impact

Kendall-Tackett (2008) proposed that developmental differences can affect children in four different impact dimensions and help provide an explanation of a sequential response over the life course:

1 *Appraisals of the victimization and its implications*—children at different stages appraise victimizations differently and tend to form different expectations based on those appraisals. Different appraisals include the child's perceptions and cognitions of the victimization in terms of self-blame, wrongness, dangerousness, a breach of moral rules, etc. For example, a 2-year-old touched sexually by an older person is likely to have a different understanding to a 10-year-old; a young person abused by an intimate partner may blame herself.

2 *Task application*—children at different stages face different developmental tasks (e.g. forming attachments, peer or intimate partner relationships) upon which these appraisals are based. For example, the understanding a young person has of an experience of child sexual abuse will affect how she approaches intimate relationships. Children who are maltreated by a caregiver in early childhood may have developed disorganized or insecure attachments and have difficulty forming relationships in later life. High levels of fear and arousal may mean a young person has a heightened sense of threat or hostility from others.

3 *Coping strategies*—children at different stages of development have different coping strategies available to them. Running away, fighting, self-harm, promiscuous sexual activity, alcohol or drug abuse are common coping strategies for adolescents. Anxiety and nightmares are more often observed in younger children. Withdrawal, avoidance or shutting down, depression and aggression or belligerent behaviour are observed in all ages. Coping strategies may change with age so that a child who is depressed and withdrawn at age 8 may use drugs to cope at age 14.

4 *Environmental buffers*—children at different stages of development operate in different family and social contexts which can alter how victimization affects them. For example, the mother's response to finding out about child sexual abuse can strongly influence the impact of the abuse on the child. Children have more negative outcomes if the mother does not believe them or blames them, or is allied to the perpetrator. Some types of abuse such as physical punishment may be 'normalized' .

(Adapted from Kendall-Tackett, 2008)

⇨

Activity

Mary lives in a large family with four siblings. Her mother and father are separated and she rarely sees her father. Her mother suffers from depression and struggles on a low income derived from welfare benefits. Mary and her siblings experience harsh physical punishment from their mother and are emotionally and physically neglected. Mary and her siblings are unpopular at school because other children say they are 'smelly'.

Consider how Kendall-Tackett's developmental dimensions model might help us understand the impact that living with abuse and neglect has upon Mary at age 3 and at age 13.

Living with domestic violence

The potential harm from exposure to domestic violence is now widely recognized in the research literature and should be taken into account in any discussion of children's experiences of living with violence.

Domestic violence is defined in England as: 'Any incident of threatening behaviour violence or abuse (psychological, physical, sexual, financial or emotional) between adults who are or have been intimate partners or family members, regardless of gender or sexuality' (Home Office, 2010). Domestic violence can be a single incident, but most often is a pattern of abusive and controlling behaviour that takes place over time in the context of a close relationship. Recognizing the experiences of adults from some ethnic groups, domestic violence is now also accepted to include forced marriage and so-called 'honour-based' violence. (The above definition takes this into account by referring to abuse not just by an intimate partner, but also by other family members). Domestic violence can occur in any relationship, heterosexual and same-sex, and both men and women can be victims. However, British Crime Survey findings show that it is women abused by male partners who most often experience repeat victimization and domestic violence that results in harm or injuries (Povey *et al.*, 2009). Research on child maltreatment and victimization in the UK found that 93.8 per cent of the perpetrators in reported cases of domestic violence were males and 2.5 per cent were females (Radford *et al.*, 2011).

Children may be adversely affected by living with domestic violence because:

- There is an overlap between violence to the parent and abuse or neglect of the child. Research on serious case reviews where children have been killed or seriously harmed has found a history of domestic violence as a significant factor linked to the child's death in two-thirds of cases (Brandon *et al.*, 2008). Research on domestic violence across the world shows that 50 to 70 per cent of children are also physically or sexually abused (Hester *et al.*, 2007). In the UK 34.4 per cent of those who reported witnessing domestic violence in childhood also reported experiences of child maltreatment (Radford *et al.*, 2011).
- Children may be hurt because they are caught in the crossfire or they intervene to protect a parent.
- Children may be harmed as a result of seeing or overhearing the domestic violence. Parents tend to underestimate just how much of the abuse their children are aware of (Mullender *et al.*, 2003). It may be especially traumatic for a child if the abusive parent resorts to forced witnessing of the abuse, or attempts to implicate or draw the children into undermining and denigrating behaviour targeted at the other parent. It is important to be aware that domestic violence may not always cease if the parents separate. In some cases the violence can get worse, especially for children involved in post-separation contact in which they may shoulder the psychological burden of having to act as a go-between, withhold information to protect a parent, or find themselves manipulated into relaying threats or reporting on another parent's activities (Radford and Hester, 2006).
- Children living with domestic violence may have to take on adult responsibilities, especially if the abuse has had an impact upon the adult victim's health. Living with domestic violence can compromise a mother's ability to parent and undermine her parenting during the relationship and post-separation, and may be an aspect of the abuser's controlling behaviour (Lapiere, 2010; Radford and Hester, 2006).
- Children's life chances may also be negatively affected by living with the fall-out of domestic violence, which can result in social isolation, poverty, homelessness and poorer educational opportunities.

Any domestic violence has the potential to adversely affect outcomes for children and young people. However, as with direct maltreatment, not everyone will be affected in the same way and research shows that having warmth and emotional support from a non-abusive parent is an important factor in a child's ability to overcome the harm caused (Hester *et al.*, 2007).

Resilience and protective factors

It should not be assumed that children and young people who live with maltreatment or victimization will inevitably experience lasting problems and poor outcomes. The impact may be immediate and harmful in the short term but ill-effects may not necessarily continue over the longer term or into adult life. Some maltreated children excel and examples of highly successful, confident adults who have spoken publicly about their difficult childhoods abound (Billy Connolly, Oprah Winfrey, etc.).

- Recent research reveals that almost half of abused children show no psychopathology in childhood and nearly one-third show no signs of mental illness in adult life (Rutter, 2007).
- Some children seem to be better able to cope with traumatic experiences than others (Haggerty et al., 1996; Rutter, 2007).
- Resilience refers to 'positive adaptation and development in the context of significant adversity' (Newman, 2004, p. 6). Resilience results from the interaction of individual characteristics and factors in the family and community that enable a person to adapt to and resist the negative impact of stress and adversity.
- Research has established a number of risks and protective factors associated with positive and negative outcomes (see Table 3.1).
- Individual factors of the child that are associated with more positive outcomes include temperament, attractiveness, personality or talents, cognitive ability, self-esteem, active coping style and social skills (Newman, 2004).
- The impact of violence and abuse may also be mitigated by having a secure relationship or attachment with an adult carer, and practical and emotional support from the wider family, from friendships or in the wider community.
- While children and young people are a strong resource and source of support for one another, informal and friendship relationships exert a hefty influence on challenging violence and sometimes also recreating the conditions that allow it to flourish (see Barter et al., 2009; Mullender et al., 2003).
- Some view educational success as an indicator of resilience, the child being able to gain self-esteem and a sense of worth and achievement through success at school (Newman, 2004). However, academic success can also indicate that the child has to comply with parental pressures to work hard or that the child is internalizing and trying to hide the experiences at home by escapism into educational perfectionism.

Reflections on the research

Is it correct to view protective factors and resilience as at the opposite end of the continuum of risk factors that operate at the individual, family and relationship, community and societal levels?

⇨

Reflections on the research—Cont'd

Coping mechanisms are thought to be the genesis of resilience (Rutter, 1996). Children are not passive responders to negative and positive environmental stimuli but actively engage with and influence the environments in which they live. The ability to problem-solve, practically and emotionally, and to reframe adversity by developing positive coping strategies and understandings of experiences plays an important part in resilience (Rutter, 1996). Research on adults coping with the consequences of childhood sexual abuse indicates that victims of abuse adopt different coping 'styles'. Adopting a 'survivor', rather than a victimized perspective on the experiences of abuse and taking a proactive approach to keeping psycho-logically and physically safe has been argued to be important in preventing re-victimization (Macy, 2007). Coping styles however cannot be considered outside the broader context of the relationships, social and environmental factors that impact upon experiences of abuse. Gender, racism, poverty and culture all play a part in a person's ability to break free from violence and abuse (Richie, 1996). Children have far more limited options to escape and mitigate the impact of abuse than do adults owing to their dependency relationship with adults. The degree to which individuals can shape or assert control over their lives is of course constrained by the options open to them and the degree of choice they have.

Children's perspectives on impact

There is surprisingly little research on the experiences and opinions of children and young adults about the consequences and impact of child maltreatment and victimization. Research on children's experiences is difficult to conduct and as a result is largely reliant on talking to children who have already been identified as experiencing maltreatment or victimization as a result of being known to the child protection services.

Research where siblings have been interviewed indicates that there are age-related differences in how children become aware of, understand and respond to living with violence and abuse (McGee, 2000; Mullender et al., 2003). What features in one sibling's account of living with violence can be less significant for another. Older children tend to have more knowledge, more resources to understand the violence, and to protect themselves and their siblings (Mullender et al., 2003). Children are not passive victims and they try to evade, avoid, 'manage' and resist abusers (McGee, 2000). In the family, children take steps to protect themselves, their siblings and often a parent (Mullender et al., 2003).

Avoidance (keeping out of the way, hiding, psychologically and emotionally blanking out), distraction (diverting the abuser's attention on to something else), intervention to protect, and providing and seeking support are some of the strategies which research shows children employ at different ages in response to living with violence and abuse (Gorin, 2004; McGee, 2000; Mudaly and Goddard, 2006; Mullender *et al.*, 2003).

Example of research—children living with domestic violence

These strategies may go together, as in the following extract from an interview with an 11-year-old boy living with domestic violence, where he describes some of the things he did to avoid the abuse, to comfort himself and his brother and to try to monitor what was happening to his mother:

> 'We would get together when T [abuser] and Mum were arguing, and cuddle up and put some music on in C's [brother's] room. When it started, I used to climb out of the window and climb back in C's window to get to C because I couldn't go out the door because they were arguing and shouting and he [abuser] was hitting and I was so frightened. Then we'd be together and we'd try to play music so we couldn't hear, but we'd still listen. Or we'd go on one of the outside roofs outside and crouch there together. And we'd stick together. Sometimes I'd cuddle up into his bed. Sometimes I'd go to sleep on the floor and then, early in the morning, before Mum woke up, I'd creep back into my own room. So no one ever knew we would do it. ... We used to cry together about it. We're very close. He looked after me.'
>
> (11-year-old boy, Mullender *et al.*, 2003, p. 125)

In Mullender *et al.*'s research half of the 45 young people living with domestic violence who were interviewed had intervened to protect the mother or siblings while half had not. It was less likely that children under the age of 12 would say they had tried to stop the violence by active intervention. However, staying awake at night to monitor and listen out for what might be happening was a common strategy reported by younger children. While some children physically intervened, especially older boys, the most common active protective strategy employed was not to get in the way of the perpetrator but to try to stop the violence by shouting, or calling the police or a neighbour to help. Children and young people take an active part in supporting one another as siblings and friends and emotionally supporting and helping the mother (Mullender *et al.*, 2003).

The perception of children living with maltreatment as reluctant or unable to talk about violence or abuse needs to be seen alongside the research on children's experiences which shows that children and young people do seek help for themselves and for others but adults do not always listen, hear them or allow them any part in decisions that are subsequently taken (Rees *et al.*, 2010; Stanley *et al.*, 2010). Although adults may be reluctant to raise sensitive issues with children because of concerns that this will be upsetting, it is evident that children and young people are able to express their views about their own experiences and the impact of living with violence and abuse and they want to be informed and involved in decisions adults make about child protection. Children in a number of studies say that what they most want is to be given information, to be treated with respect by adults, to be included in decisions about what might happen and not be kept in the dark (Cossar *et al.*, 2011; Gorin, 2004; McGee, 2000; Mullender *et al.*, 2003; Stanley *et al.*, 2010).

Reflections on the research

Question: Children most often turn to peers and siblings for support, comfort and protection when living with violence and abuse. What are the implications for public education and awareness activities?

How can adults best support children and young people to care for one another?

Summary of key points

- Victimization and maltreatment in childhood can have short-term and lasting adverse consequences for health, mental health and well-being that continue into adulthood.
- It is the emotional and psychological impact of victimization rather than the physical injuries which most often debilitates and disadvantages individuals.
- In the context of developmental and structured dependency, where there are material and emotional ties between the perpetrator and victim, victimization and maltreatment can be difficult for the person affected to name and to position as abusive.
- Children and young people who experience physical violence, child maltreatment or sexual abuse are vulnerable to re-victimization and to polyvictimization so that they experience victimization at home, in the school and in the community. Children who are polyvictims have the highest levels of trauma impact.
- Almost half of all maltreated children show no psychopathology in childhood and nearly one-third show no signs of mental ill-health in adulthood.
- Children's ability to overcome adversity and trauma varies according to

the interaction between individual, family and community factors that are protective assets (coping strategies, emotional and social support, the availability of love and care from an adult, etc.) or vulnerabilities, risks and disadvantages.

- Emotional support, friendships, sense of self-worth and achievement and adopting a 'survivor' perspective are important aspects in overcoming adversity and trauma.
- Research with children and young people shows that there are barriers to disclosure; however, when children do tell adults, adults do not always hear, listen or act appropriately, and this can increase feelings of isolation, stigma and powerlessness.

Further reading

Howe, D. (2005) *Child Abuse and Neglect: Attachment, Development and Intervention*. London: Palgrave Macmillan.

Reviews the impact of abuse and neglect, illustrating the analysis with a number of case study examples drawn from research and practice.

Mudaly, C. and Goddard, C. (2006) *The Truth is Longer than a Lie: Children's Experiences of Abuse and Professional Interventions*. London: JKP.

A qualitative study of young survivors, experiences of child maltreatment and professional interventions in Australia.

Mullender, A., Hague, G., Inman, U., Kelly, L., Malos, E. and Regan, L. (2003) *Children's Perspectives on Domestic Violence*. London: Sage.

Research on children's experiences of living with domestic violence towards their mothers based on interviews with children in contact with domestic violence services.

Research details

Polyvictimization—Finkelhor *et al.*, 2005b

Telephone interviews in the USA with a nationally representative sample of caregivers of children aged 2 to 9 years and young people aged 10 to 17. Some 2,030 caregivers and young people were interviewed about their own/their child's experiences of victimization. The researchers investigated associations between trauma symptom scores and different types of victimization and polyvictimization.

Finkelhor, D., Ormrod, D., Turner, H. and Hamby, S. (2005b) Measuring polyvictimization using the Juvenile Victimization Questionnaire. *Child Abuse and Neglect* 29, 1297–1312.

Young people's views on maltreatment—Mudaly and Goddard (2006)
An in-depth study based on interviews with nine young people aged 9 to 18 who had been maltreated in childhood. Young people were recruited through a therapy centre in Western Australia. Their caregivers were also interviewed.

Mudaly, C. and Goddard, C. (2006) *The Truth is Longer than a Lie: Children's Experiences of Abuse and Professional Interventions*. London: JKP.

Children with child protection plans—Cossar *et al.* (2011)
Interviews with 26 children with child protection plans were conducted in their homes for the Office of the Children's Commissioner.

Cossar, A., Brandon, M. and Jordan, P. (2011) *Don't Make Assumptions; Children and Young People's Views of the Child Protection System and Messages for Change*. London: Office of the Children's Commissioner (www.childrens commissioner.gov.uk).

Children living with domestic violence—Mullender *et al.* (2003)
Forty-five children and young people between the ages of 8 and 18 were interviewed as well as their mothers about their experiences of living with domestic violence. The mothers and children were recruited from domestic violence refuges and community-based services.

Mullender, A., Hague, G., Inman, U., Kelly, L., Malos, E. and Regan, L. (2003) *Children's Perspectives on Domestic Violence*. London: Sage.

Villains and Victims

Introduction and key questions

This chapter looks at public attitudes towards violence, the framing of childhood violence in the media and the consequences for children's lives. Questions considered in this chapter will be:

- Why are public attitudes about young people and violence at odds with current trends?
- What part do the media play in childhood violence?

Public attitudes towards violence and children

Tracking of public attitudes towards crime and antisocial behaviour show that a (now smaller) gap exists between public perceptions of crime and antisocial behaviour and actual levels recorded by police or by the British Crime Survey.

Examples of research: The reality gap in public perceptions of youth behaviour

- Parent reports on their teenage children's antisocial behaviour (including lying, stealing and disobedience) increased throughout the 1970s, 1980s and 1990s before falling slightly in the 2000s (HM Government, 2009).
- Smoking and cannabis use by young people declined in the 10 years up until 2009 but alcohol consumption by 11- to 15-year-olds doubled and the proportion of English and Welsh 15-year-olds who report having ever been drunk is twice the rate reported in other European countries (HM Government, 2009).
- Sixty-six per cent of those interviewed for the British Crime Survey 2009 to 2010 believed overall crime to be increasing, 90 per cent believed knife crime had increased nationally, while 81 per cent thought gun crime had risen, whereas reported incidents of gun crime declined by 3 per cent in 2009–2010 and injuries caused by sharp implements fell by 4 per cent (Flatley *et al.*, 2010).
- Longer term trends from the BCS show that since 1995, the number of violent incidents has fallen by half (50%) and in 2009 to 2010 were at a similar level to 1981 (Flatley *et al.*, 2010).
- Although rates of concern among adults about youth 'hanging around' the streets have declined, 27 per cent of adults still report this as being a major worry in their neighbourhoods (Flatley *et al.*, 2010).

Reflections on the research

Activity 1

How do you reconcile public perceptions of high rates of juvenile crime with the research evidence on young people, crime and violence discussed in Chapter 2, pp. 30–33?

Activity 2

What might be the factors that influence public perceptions of youth crime?

The media and childhood violence

Research suggests that factors associated with public perceptions of high crime rates include being a reader of a 'popular' rather than broadsheet newspaper (Duffy *et al.*, 2008), being employed and over the age of 75 (Flatley *et al.*, 2010). Adults are the majority of those responsible for anti social behaviour (Home Office, 2009b) but it is young people's behaviour that makes the news and most often it is 'prolific offenders' who are featured. Public perceptions of children as 'villains' or 'victims' are influenced by the media's sensationalist reporting on rare events such as child homicides, sex murders and extreme cases of child abuse. Press reports on crime and violence are staples for the news but reports have increased in post-war Britain from being 10 per cent of the stories in *The Times* and *Daily Mail* in the 1940s to 20 per cent of stories covered in the 1990s (Reiner, 2007).

Half of British adults are scared of children who 'behave like feral animals'

Half of British adults believe children's behaviour has descended to the level of feral animals, a survey revealed today.

The charity Barnardo's found that Britons are increasingly frightened of the younger generation and believe them to be a danger to each other and adults.

A poll of more than 2,000 adults found that 54 per cent believe British children are 'beginning to behave like animals'.

Plague: Adults have likened children to 'feral animals' and 'vermin' who have 'infested' the streets of Britain.

A similar proportion agreed that children are sometimes referred to as 'feral' because this is the way they conduct themselves.

More than a third of respondents likened children to vermin, warning that the streets were 'infested' with them.

The findings sparked claims that escalating youth crime and a wave of horrific stabbings were taking their toll on the public's perception of children.

Latest figures from the Youth Justice Board show that crimes against the person committed by 10 to 17-year-olds are up by 39 per cent in three years. These range from common assault to murder.

Almost 300,000 crimes of any kind were committed by under-18s in 2006/07, with boys responsible for 235,893 and girls 59,236.

(*Daily Mail*, 2008)

Activity 1

What messages about children and violence are given by this extract from the Daily Mail?

⇨

Half of British adults are scared of children who 'behave like feral animals'—Cont'd

Activity 2

Does the extract help or hinder public understanding of adults' attitudes towards children and young people?

Child victims in the media

'You know they suffer and do nothing'—Action for Children media campaign on child neglect, showing a small, sad and lonely-looking, blonde-haired girl sitting on concrete steps holding a rag doll (Action for Children, 2009).

'Miles is a quiet baby who learnt that nobody comes whether he cries or not ... Sometimes we need to open our eyes to the suffering all around us'—NSPCC TV advertisement showing a silently crying toddler standing in his cot in a dark room (NSPCC, 2007).

'The child sits limp and despairing—her face hidden in her hands; the young girl clutches her blanket—the figure of a man lurks in the shadows; an infant cowers in the corner of his playpen, a blank-eyed Victorian china doll lies cracked and discarded on the floor. These are the images which appear in the publicity about, and campaigns against, child sexual abuse. They are used by people who are outraged by the abuse of children and are seeking to prevent it' (Kitzinger, 1997, p.165).

Activity

- Think about the imagery invoked by the last news report or campaign advert on child abuse you saw, heard or read.
- Make a list of the features of the report or campaign advert that make it 'newsworthy' or 'important'.
- Now repeat the same exercise, thinking about the imagery invoked by the last news report you saw, heard or read on violence committed by children and young people.
- Compare the two lists of 'newsworthy' or 'important' features. What are the similarities and differences?

Violence by and towards children is often newsworthy. Essential elements of a 'good story' include some of the following.

Topic-related interest:

- a celebrity;
- an unusual event happening to an 'ordinary', preferably appealing, person;
- crime or violence;
- sex and titilation (Greer, 2007).

'Framing' of the elements of the story to create:

- an 'innocent' victim;
- someone to blame;
- moral judgement on the causes, people responsible or impact of the problem;
- a simple message or easy solution (Nichols, 2011).

Babies are at the top of the media victimization hierarchy because they fit perfectly with the simplified construction of an innocent victim. Remember the image of baby Peter Connelly, a small, blond-haired, blue-eyed boy holding up his arm as if pleading to be held, picked up and comforted. Three-year-old Ryan Lovell-Hancox, also tortured and neglected by his two drug-addicted stand-in 'carers', was similarly shown in the press as a smiling, blond-haired, blue-eyed toddler in his bathrobe (*Daily Mail*, 2011). Alongside both children the press printed images of a computer-generated hairless child manikin showing the numerous injuries on the child's head and body found at the time of death. The murder of baby Peter Connelly brought a tsunami of public outrage against social workers who 'failed to act', self-obsessed mothers who failed to care and men who were sadistic, cruel 'monsters' who gained pleasure in torturing innocent small children behind closed doors. Visual, written and aural cues in media imagery on child abuse accentuate the vulnerable and passive features of children as innocent victims, dependent on 'decent' adults doing something to help (Kitzinger, 1997).

Violent youth in contrast are older children, 'feral' youth hanging about on the streets, engaging in mindless violence, vandalism, gang violence, drug-taking, or drinking and terrorizing 'decent' people. Violent youth are usually hoodied boys, although girls can hide their sexuality behind the hoodie. The media have promoted stories about antisocial white youth mobs or young black male gangs in inner cities, morally condemned for being the no-hoper offspring of absent fathers and disinterested or incompetent single mothers, with nothing better to do but seek gratification from behaving badly.

Activity

Would adding information from research done with young people about their experiences of violence alter the representation of children as 'villains' or 'victims'? Reread the circumstances and characteristics of young offenders on pages 33 and the risk factors associated with criminal behaviour discussed on pages 46–47 and consider this question with reference to the media extract on 'feral children' on page 101.

Examples from research—Media contributions to crime

Rob Reiner looked at historical trends in news media crime reporting in post war Britain, comparing reports in broadsheets such as *The Times* with tabloids such as the *Daily Mail*. Reiner argued that for a crime to occur there are several necessary pre-conditions—labelling, motive, means, opportunities and absence of controls. The media potentially plays a part in each of these.

- *Labelling*—Behaviour needs to be named or labelled as offensive. The media help shape conceptual boundaries and can play an important role in creating new perceptions of crime. For example, the media were influential in creating moral panic about the crime 'mugging', violent street robbery by black male youth in the 1980s (Hall *et al.*, 1980). The media can also help raise awareness about crimes and the need for better responses. For example, in 1982 a fly-on-the-wall documentary TV programme was made on Thames Valley Police responses to rape victims. This resulted in campaigns to bring better treatment of rape victims by the police (Gregory and Lees, 1999).
- *Motive*—The media present universal images of common lifestyles which influence aspirations and feelings of anomie or relative deprivation, or perceptions of injustice which may motivate crime or create conditions for social learning (see research discussed in Chapter 2).
- *Means*—The media spread knowledge about criminal and abusive techniques. For example, the 10-year-old boys who killed James Bulger were said to have drawn upon knowledge gained from watching the video *Child's Play 3* during their ritualized abuse and dismemberment of the child.
- *Opportunity*—The media can influence people's routine activities and how they spend their leisure time, thereby also influencing opportunities for crime.
- *Absence of controls*—The media can glamorize violent and abusive behaviour, relaxing control and inhibitions.

Although research shows strong statistical associations between exposure to violent, criminal or sexualized materials and subsequent abusive and criminal behaviour, it is difficult to show conclusively the extent of any direct causal link because other factors apart from the media have an influence. This means that media exposure could have a lot or not much influence.

(Reiner, 2007, pp. 302–337)

Commercial interests to get a good story and generate sales and income can tempt journalists to ignore people's rights and even commit acts that are criminal. The public were shocked by information on phone hacking by *News of the World* reporters that came out after the trial of the killer of 13-year-old Millie Dowler in 2011. To get a 'good story' reporters had hacked into Millie's mobile phone messages shortly after her disappearance, even before her body had been found. Subsequent investigations brought to light other hacking activities, and the closure of the *News of the World* followed. The media sensationalize experiences and victimize children so that distorted, partial or unbalanced accounts are given that frequently neglect to give children themselves any voice.

News media can influence what happens and what we know. Educating the public about child abuse and neglect has always been a crucial aspect of campaigning for change for organizations working to improve children's lives and well-being. Publicity given to young people's experiences of sexual abuse by Esther Rantzen's *That's Life* TV programme in the 1980s brought to life ChildLine, the UK's confidential advice line for children and young people. The media can play an important part in challenging and changing public attitudes towards children and young people and in promoting children's rights to be safe.

Activity

In the UK in 2000 to 2001, in response to the murder of an 8-year-old schoolgirl, The *News of the World* led a campaign to publicly name men who appeared on the sex abusers register. As part of its campaign, each week the newspaper named some of the men living in the community. The campaign divided public opinion. Some families were angry that they had not been informed that they were living close to known paedophiles, but some police and social workers said that naming people on the register caused them to 'go underground' so that they could no longer be monitored. The campaign also led to some of the wrong people being targeted as vigilantes hurled stones at the homes of suspected child sex offenders (IFJ, 2002, p. 38).
Question: What messages about the risks of child victimization are presented by the *News of the World* campaign? Consider how these risks of children being killed and sexually abused compare with what is known from research about the risks of child victimization (see Chapters 1 and 3).

Portraying children as victims or villains can do more harm than good, fuelling adult prejudices, treating children as ciphers for adult emotions rather than citizens in their own right. Consider the baby Miles campaign, illustrated above in the fundraising campaign by a children's charity. The message presented is that neglected children are helpless, very young and easy to spot (baby Miles is crying alone quietly in a darkened room, with no one to comfort him). We cannot ask baby Miles about his experiences of neglect because he is too young to express a view. The simple message of the victimized child with a simple solution (donate to a charity so that baby Miles can be rescued) provides no contextualized information from research about child neglect to tell us about the older children and young people who are also affected, who are not 'easy' to spot and may be resentful of adult intrusion into their families (Stein *et al.*, 2009). Promoting the view that child neglect is easy to spot 'if only we open our eyes' misleads the public into the false belief that there are simple solutions and helps fuel the blame directed at social workers who 'fail' to see a child at risk of dying (see discussion of the media and social work in Eileen Munro's review of child protection: Munro, 2010, 2011a, 2011b).

Kitzinger (1997) has argued that the glorification of victimized children as innocents has a fetishistic nature that does nothing to challenge a sex abuser's attraction towards children and the exploitation of seeking titillation from human misery. The child who cannot be positioned so easily as 'innocent' because she is older, or more knowing, who has fought or answered back, or the child who is just less 'visually appealing' to adults becomes the less deserving victim. The sensationalist media coverage of stabbings and gang crime has, according to the Home Office, partly contributed to an 'arms race' in knife carrying for protective purposes among young people living in some inner city areas (House of Commons, 2009). It contributes to fear and inter-generational barriers between youth and older people (Flatley *et al.*, 2010). The simplified dichotomy of children and young people into either victims or villains can help disguise the fact that some are both. It masks children's agency and resistance to abuse and neglect, aggravating the tendency for adults to position the troubled child as troublesome.

Activity

Taking an approach informed by the United Nations Convention on the Rights of the Child (UNCRC), in 2002 the International Federation of Journalists published guidance on the media and children. These state:

Journalists and media organizations shall strive to maintain the highest standards of ethical conduct in reporting children's affairs and, in particular, they shall:

1 **strive** for standards of excellence in terms of accuracy and sensitivity when reporting on issues involving children;
2 **avoid** programming and publication of images which intrude upon the media space of children with information which is damaging to them;
3 **avoid** the use of stereotypes and sensational presentation to promote journalistic material involving children;
4 **consider** carefully the consequences of publication of any material concerning children and minimize harm to children;
5 **guard** against visually or otherwise identifying children unless it is demonstrably in the public interest;
6 **give** children, where possible, the right of access to media to express their own opinions without inducement of any kind;
7 **ensure** independent verification of information provided by children and take special care to ensure that verification takes place without putting child informants at risk;
8 **avoid** the use of sexualized images of children;
9 **use** fair, open and straightforward methods for obtaining pictures and, where possible, obtain them with the knowledge and consent of children or a responsible adult, guardian or carer;
10 **verify** the credentials of any organization purporting to speak for or to represent the interests of children;
11 **not** make payment to children for material involving the welfare of children or to parents or guardians of children unless it is demonstrably in the interest of the child.

Journalists should put to critical examination the reports submitted and the claims made by Governments on implementation of the UN Convention on the Rights of the Child in their respective countries.

Media should not consider and report the conditions of children only as events but should continuously report the process likely to lead or leading to the occurrence of these events.

(IFJ, 2002, p. 63)

1 Is it possible to have a 'good story' or an effective campaigning message on children and violence without the essential and framing elements described on pages 102–3?
2 Consider the guidelines from the IFJ with reference to the reports on violent children on page 101. If the guidelines were applied, would the story change? Would there still be a 'good story'?
3 Can you think of a media report on children's experiences of violence, whether as instigators or as victims, that took an informative approach, gave children's views respectfully, was not sensationalist and did not exploit or victimize children?
4 Are media representations of children and violence more reflections of 'respectable fears' (Reiner, 2007) about children than justifications for their social control and surveillance?

Summary

- Research shows that the general public perceive the youth rates of violence, crime and antisocial behaviour to be higher than the rates reported to the British Crime Survey.
- The media and campaigning organizations have influenced public perceptions of violence and young people by focusing on rare and sensationalist events such as homicides or extreme cases of child abuse.
- Representations of children and young people as victims or villains has consequences for the well-being of children and young people—their experiences of violence are misrepresented, and over-simplified accounts of the causes and consequences hinder progress in policy and practice.

Further reading

Kitzinger, J. (1997) 'Who are you kidding? Children, power and the struggle against sexual abuse', in James, A. and Prout, A. (eds) *Constructing and Re Constructing Childhood,* (2nd edn) London: Routledge (pp. 165–189).

A thoughtful analysis of media representations of child victims from a childhood studies perspective.

Research details

British Crime Survey

The British Crime Survey is an annual survey of a representative sample of adults and children living in households in England and Wales. About 37,000 adults are interviewed. The survey was extended to cover children aged 10 to 15 in 2009, when 3,661 children and young people were interviewed after their parent had completed the adult survey.

Various publications on the survey are available. For the most recent survey see Chaplin, R., Flatley, J. and Smith, K. (2011) *Crime in England and Wales 2010–11.* London: Home Office (www.homeoffice.gov.uk).

Media and Crime—Reiner 2007

A review of published research on crime reporting including Reiner's own research. Reiner conducted a content analysis of crime reports post-war looking at reporting in tabloid press and broadsheets 1945 to 1991.

Reiner, R. (2007) 'Media made criminality: The representation of crime in the mass media', in Maguire, M., Morgan, R. and Reiner, R. (eds) *The Oxford Handbook of Criminology* 575–601. Oxford: Oxford University Press (pp. 302–337).

Behaving Badly

Chapter Outline

Introduction and key questions

This chapter looks at the framing of childhood violence in crime prevention policies in public and cyberspace and the consequences for children's lives.

Questions considered in this chapter will be:

- Have policies designed to treat young offenders differently helped or hindered violence prevention?
- What impact do adult fears about danger in public spaces have on the well-being of children and young people?
- How has the commercialization and sexualization of childhood affected children and young people and their use of information technology to network and communicate?

Youth justice and public policy

Have policies designed to treat young offenders differently helped or hindered violence prevention?

The media positioning of children as villains has also been cynically exploited by politicians to create a punitive approach to young offenders in public policy. This has done little to help them overcome the consequences of living with violence.

Government policy on crime and young people has long recognized that child offenders should be treated differently to adults. A separate system of juvenile justice existed in England since the Children Act 1908 created the juvenile court and barred children aged under 14 from prison (Morgan and Newburn, 2007). Juvenile justice has historically addressed both *justice*, the desire to punish, imprison and contain offenders, and *welfare* principles, recognizing the young person's need for education to help them reform. Welfare approaches resist labelling young people too soon as convicted criminals because, as argued in Chapter 2, many will 'grow out of crime'. Custody is a last resort, used for the most serious offences when other options for reform or re-education have been exhausted. Justice principles favour conviction and custody to punish offenders and protect society. The relative emphasis on welfare and justice in public policy has shifted over time.

The high tide of welfarism is generally accepted as being encapsulated in the Children and Young Persons Act 1969, although the Act was never fully implemented, as a new government was elected the following year. The Act established the idea that the justice system was to be a last resort for juveniles, favoured diversion out of custody and re-education and rehabilitation of young offenders. It abolished approved schools and remand homes, and replaced them with residential and educational homes. The emphasis on keeping young people out of custody was held up until the 1990s. The Conservative government in the 1980s had a brief experiment with 'short, sharp, shock' approaches to custody for young offenders but found little evidence to show that boot camps helped prevent crime (Morgan and Newburn, 2007). The 1982 Criminal Justice Act limited the use of custody for young offenders and provided alternative sentencing options, such as supervision orders or intensive treatment. Young offenders were diverted from being labelled too readily with convictions by the use of police cautions.

A shift in emphasis came with the moral panic about violent children that followed the abduction and killing in 1993 of 2-year-old James Bulger by the 10-year-old boys, Robert Thompson and John Venables. The then prime minister, John Major, signalled the start of a backlash against being 'soft' on young offenders by claiming that the time had come for 'society to condemn a little more and understand a little less' (Goldson, 2002). The policy to reduce the number of young offenders in custody was reversed. The Criminal Justice and Public Order Act 1994 doubled the sentence that could be given to 15- to 17-year-olds for young offender institutions to two years. Parents became bound to ensure a young person carried out a community sentence. Secure Training Orders were introduced for offenders aged 12 to 14 and five secure training centres were built. The numbers of young people in custody rose by 122 per cent between 1993 and 1999 (Morgan and Newburn, 2007) so that England and Wales had rates of locking up children and young people that were higher than many countries in Western Europe (Natale, 2010).

The Labour government, elected in 1997 with Tony Blair's promise to be 'tough on crime and on the causes of crime', indicated that 'Third Way' policies on juvenile crime would not waiver from increasingly punitive action. The Labour government policy on being tough on young people's crime involved increasing use of custody and, instead of diversion, control, surveillance and monitoring of children and their families. There was net widening by expanding the focus beyond children who broke the law to include those vulnerable to doing so and tackling their antisocial behaviour. The Crime and Disorder Act 1998 introduced antisocial behaviour orders (ASBOs), child safety orders and local child curfew orders which could be made for a minimum period of two years.

The Crime and Disorder Act set the foundation for Labour's top-down, central government-driven and managerialist approach to crime reduction, which required strategic multi-agency planning, target-setting and performance management at national and local levels. The Act set up the Youth Justice Board, which was to create performance measures on reducing young people's crime, monitor national standards for youth justice, conduct research, promote good practice and advise ministers. At the local authority level multi-agency Youth Offending Teams (YOTs) were established to target young offenders and intervene. Cautions were replaced with a new reprimand and final warning approach. Those who were given a final warning were referred to the YOT to take part in rehabilitation activities.

Spending on youth justice increased by 45 per cent in the first ten years of the Labour government term. In 2000 the Youth Justice Board took on responsibility to commission services that included places in the secure estate. The Youth Justice Board invested in prevention activities and intensive supervision and surveillance programmes as alternatives to custody, but over ten times more was spent on custody than on prevention, and evidence of impact was mixed (Solomon and Garside, 2008). Lack of clarity about objectives for different interventions that developed and a proliferation of conflicting objectives are seen to have undermined progress (HM Government, 2009). The numbers of young people in custody grew at first but by 2008 were again falling, although those on remand currently still make up 28 per cent of young offenders in custody (Ministry of Justice, 2011).

Violent crime was identified as a specific concern in the Home Office strategy *Cutting Crime 2008–11*, where intentions for early intervention, preventing escalation and being robust in criminal justice responses were reaffirmed (Home Office, 2008). The Youth Crime Action Plan launched in 2008 aimed for a comprehensive and tough approach to enforcement, non-negotiable support and challenge for young people and their families, and better and earlier preventive interventions (HM Government, 2008b). To route young offenders into the most appropriate intervention early on, triage systems were established where members of a YOT team worked closely with the police to review and determine responses to cases at an earlier point. Street-based teams and mentoring systems, location of police in schools to promote community safety via 'Safer Schools' and intensive supervision were some of the many initiatives set up. Non-negotiable 'supportive' responses to antisocial behaviour included parenting contracts and drawing families with children with antisocial behaviour into intervention programmes such as the Family Intervention Projects (FIPs), set up in 2006. The FIPs were aimed at families with antisocial behaviour at high risk of having poorer outcomes owing to a combination of difficulties such as substance misuse, mental health problems, learning difficulties, housing problems, unemployment, poor school attendance, debt and domestic violence. FIPs could be provided as an intensive outreach/home visiting package, through a 'dispersed service' (where the family were put into temporary accommodation while involved with FIPs) or as a 'core unit service' (where the family was accommodated and supervised for 24 hours a day). Because of these compulsory accommodation elements, the media and some criminologists described FIPs as 'sin bins' for problem families (Gregg, 2010). FIPs workers provided a range of services including access to advice, support and parenting programmes to tackle the family's difficulties. A mixture of sanctions and support encouraged parents to stay involved. Sanctions for failing to cooperate with the FIPs team included loss of tenancy (if in social housing) or taking children into local authority care.

Changing behaviour through family intervention
Activity

- Much of the alleged ASB of FIPs families involved social inadequacy and mental health issues.
- Eighty per cent of families had mental/physical health problems and learning disabilities.
- Sixty per cent were found to be 'victims of ASB' and described as 'easily scape-goated' in disputes by project managers.
- Fifty-nine per cent of the adults had clinical depression and anxiety problems.
- Fifty-four per cent of families had one or more children with a mental or physical disability.
- Seventy-two per cent were lone-mother families.
- Eighty-five per cent of adults were unemployed.
- Fifty-nine per cent of families were in debt.

These are chronic problems, not lifestyle choices. Across the FIPs, over ten years, we are dealing not with 'families from hell' but with 'families in hell' with little hope of escape. Yet the level of medical support given in the projects is totally inadequate, and parenting classes do not treat mental health problems.

(Gregg, 2010)

Were FIPs targeted more at the symptoms than the causes of the families' difficulties?

Youth Rehabilitation Orders
Activity

The Youth and Crime Commission Consultation Report published in 2009 shows the complicated array of initiatives that developed under Labour to deal with young crime and antisocial behaviour (HM Government, 2009). The interventions that developed were costly and the most resource intensive were not necessarily more effective (HM Government, 2009). In 2009 a generic Youth Rehabilitation Order (YRO) was intro-duced in England and Wales for non-custodial sentences. This drew together existing community-based sentences and requirements into one 'wraparound' order. Sentencers could select components from a menu of 18 different requirements: ⇨

- Participation in constructive activities
- A curfew
- Exclusion from specified places
- Local authority residence
- School attendance and other education requirements
- Mental health treatment
- Unpaid work (16 and 17-year-olds)
- Drug testing
- Intoxicating substance treatment
- Supervision
- Monitoring by electronic 'tag'
- Prohibited activities
- Drug treatment
- Residence
- Participation in specified programmes
- Going to an attendance centre at specified times
- Intensive supervision and surveillance
- Intensive fostering

All offenders were incorporated into a scaled approach of increasingly intense supervision and monitoring to match the likelihood of re-offending and the risk of serious harm to others. The scaled approach was to offer a range of options relevant to the needs of the offender and the victim.

Consider the range of available options for community sentences. What is the balance between support, rehabilitation, 'pay back' to the community and control?

What are the possible benefits from these options for victims of crime?

There are mixed views about the achievements of the Labour government approach (Downes, 2010). The numbers of children and young people in custody fell from 2006. In 2006 to 2007 the average number of under-18-year-olds in custody at any one time was 2,914, and in 2010 to 2011 it was 2,067, a decline of 29 per cent. The biggest change was for 10- to 14-year olds where the number in custody at any one time was 196 in 2006 to 2007 and 96 in 2010 to 2011, a fall of 51 per cent (Ministry of Justice, 2011). Keeping children and young people locked up is expensive and it was felt that local authorities had no incentive to bring the numbers down as the YJB carried the costs for giving them 'respite' from the most troublesome young people (Brookes *et al.*, 2010).

Between 2000 and 2008, the frequency of re-offending fell by 15.9 per cent. The frequency of re-offending for young males aged 18 to 20 fell by 32 per cent over that time period, and the likelihood of them committing at least one re-offence in 2010 was less than 50 per cent (HM Government, 2010c). However, 75 per cent of young people released from custody and 68 per cent of young people on community sentences re-offend within a year (Ministry of Justice, 2010c), indicating that these forms of punishment were ineffective in preventing further crime.

Mixed objectives from the range of initiatives made it hard to produce evidence about what was effective (HM Government, 2009). Low-level offenders were thought to escalate too quickly into the criminal justice system owing to the rigid reprimand and final warning approach (Ministry of Justice, 2010c). There were concerns that ASBOs did little to stop young people misbehaving in public as half the ASBOS issued since 2002 were breached (Home Office, 2010). ASBOs had a net widening effect, driving more young people towards criminal convictions at a younger age (Solomon and Garside, 2008).

Others believed too little emphasis had been given to risk factors and interventions known from research to be effective, including restorative justice approaches (Police Foundation, 2010). While efforts had been made via programmes such as FIPs to work with families, only just over 3,000 families had completed FIPs programmes by 2010 (NATCEN, 2010). The evidence of the success of FIPs was also questioned on the grounds that it was based mainly on professional rather than service users' views about effectiveness and no comparison group had ever been used to compare results and outcomes (Gregg, 2010).

The coalition government published a Green Paper *Breaking the Cycle* in 2010 (Ministry of Justice, 2010c). This set out plans to shift power from central government to local people and increase the accountability of police via publicly elected Police and Crime Commissioners to drive local priorities for tackling crime. For youth crime the focus stayed on tackling the risk factors for offending but doing this by developing stronger community engagement, improving the effectiveness of sentencing, including expecting young offenders to pay back for the harm caused (Home Affairs Committee, 2011). The coalition government also aimed to promote prevention. Abolition of the Youth Justice Board was announced as part of the drive towards local control over priorities. Incentives were announced for local services and partnerships to reduce offending and re-offending in the form of a payment by results system (Ministry of Justice, 2010c). Parenting support, parenting programmes and parenting orders, focusing mostly on mothers, remained part of the prevention and early intervention approach and sat well with the government intention to roll back responsibility on to communities to create the Big Society.

Diversion from custody was to be achieved by making local authorities carry the costs of custody and rewards of finding workable alternatives. A funding stream for alternatives to custody, the Justice Reinvestment Pathfinder Initiative, was announced in 2010 and pilot schemes were established with YOTs to test ways of creating incentives and responsibilities for carrying the costs of custody.

At the time of writing it is too soon to see what the impact of these policies will be. Prevention and whole community approaches (discussed further in Chapter 7) however depend on creating resources at a local level to address the fundamental inequalities that lie at the root of violence and crime. Demonstrating that preventive activities are successful also takes time and it will be a challenge for local partnerships to develop the evidence needed to show success and secure funds to reward these efforts. A less fragmented approach to young offenders is needed that takes into account the research (discussed in Chapter 2) on victimized and victimizing young people.

Danger and nuisance in public space and cyberspace

What impact do adult fears about danger in public spaces have upon the well-being of children and young people? Children's lives have been affected by media and public policy restricting their access to public space through ASBOs and other surveillance policies to rid the streets of groups of youths.

Moving On Mosquitoes

Howard Stapleton is the inventor of an electronic device called the 'Mosquito' which was designed to deter young people from hanging around outside shops. The mosquito, first produced in 2005, emits a painful high-frequency sound that is audible only to people under the age of 25. Five thousand Mosquito devices are thought to have been sold in England and Wales to shopkeepers and police forces (*Guardian*, 2010). In June 2010 the human rights group Liberty asked the European Council for Human Rights to rule on whether or not the devices should be banned but apart from issuing a statement that they should be discouraged there has been a reluctance to become involved.

Example of research—use of public space

Findings from the British Crime Survey of 10- to 15-year-olds 2009–2010:

- Eighty-one per cent of 10 to 15 year olds said they hang around public spaces.
- Fifty-two per cent do this at least once a week.
- Boys (25%) are more likely to hang around public spaces than are girls (17%).
- One in five (20%) of 10- to 15-year-olds were moved on when hanging out with friends.
- Members of the public were most likely to move young people on (41%).
- Thirty-five per cent of 10- to 15-year-olds felt that teenagers hanging around public spaces was a problem, compared with 27 per cent of adults who saw this as a problem.
- Forty-five per cent of 10- to 15-year-olds in socially deprived areas saw teenagers hanging around in public as being a problem.
- Fifty-nine per cent of 10- to 15-year-olds thought there were enough activities for young people of their age in their neighbourhood.
- Eighty-four per cent of 10- to 15-year-olds said that parks and playgrounds were available, and 62 per cent said they used them.

(Hoare *et al.*, 2011)

Young people, both boys and girls, have been increasingly reported as 'menaces' in public spaces when they gather in groups and loitering youths are banned from public areas or subject to regulation in malls. Adult fears about children and young people in public spaces has led to regulation over their movements (see Chapter 1). There have been restrictions as well through private enterprise activities, particularly the impact of property development and building on the lack of availability of green spaces where children can play or hang out in cities.

Example of research—playing outdoors

New research from Savlon and Play England reveals that two-thirds of parents always had adventures outdoors as a child but worry that their children do not have the same opportunities today.

Many parents' fondest childhood memories are of playing outside; however, outdoor activities that for parents were part of growing up seem to be in danger of disappearing:

- Forty-two per cent of children report they have never made a daisy-chain.
- Thirty-two per cent have never climbed a tree.
- A quarter of children today have never had the simple pleasure of rolling down a hill.
- Forty-seven per cent of adults built dens every week as a child, yet 29 per cent of today's children say they have never built a den.
- One-third of children have never played hopscotch.
- One in ten children have never ridden a bike. ⇨

> The research confirms parents' concerns that children are no longer spending their time playing outdoors. Seventy-two per cent of adults played outside rather than indoors, compared to 40 per cent of children today, with children now at risk of losing out on essential childhood experiences that outdoor play brings (www.playengland.org.uk/news, 8 July 2011).

Lack of access to safe places to play and for leisure activities carries potential of harm to children's health. Play is essential for child development; it is how infants and toddlers learn about themselves and the world. Play is vitally important in providing the very young with the experiences they need in order to develop the language, social and cognitive skills that will serve them throughout life but concerns have been raised by a number of children's organizations and researchers about the increased restrictions on the time and space available to allow children's play, especially in inner city areas where finding safe places in which to play can be increasingly difficult (DEMOS, 2007). Play can have therapeutic benefits for children (and probably for adults too), although play-based therapies have had less attention in evaluation research than other approaches (Fonagy *et al.*, 2002). To restrict an infant or toddler's capacity to play is to restrict their cognitive and social development.

Reflections on the research
Activity 1
Does the research suggest less use of public spaces by children and young people or does it show that children and young people use public spaces and leisure facilities but are more likely to be seen as nuisances and get moved on?

Activity 2
Are adults less tolerant of young people's behaviour in public?
A frequently played game in my own childhood was to knock on people's doors and run away and hide before the adult inside opened the door to see who was there. Is 'being naughty' antisocial behaviour?

Activity 3
Are children expected to be inside more today than was previously the case?

Risk and danger in cyberspace

Regulations, risks and preferences have brought children indoors, communicating more with others in a virtual world. In the virtual world there is little regulation, age can be obscured and adults are fearful of the risks to children, especially to girls, from exposure to age-inappropriate adult material or to exploitation by inappropriate adults.

How has the commercialization and sexualization of childhood affected children and young people and their use of information technology to network and communicate?

Examples of research
Sexual victimization in Europe

A comparative study of sexual abuse, selling sex and use of pornography among 11,528 18-year-olds from Norway, Sweden, Lithuania, Estonia and Poland found that 93.1 per cent of boys and 71.7 per cent of girls had accessed pornography; 6.8 per cent of boys (9.4 per cent in Sweden) and 0.1 per cent of girls accessed pornography daily. Young people reported high rates of sexual victimization of others. Between 24.2 per cent (Estonia) and 9.7 per cent (Norway) of boys had dragged, persuaded, pressed or forced someone into sexual activities. Between 10.5 per cent (Estonia) and 1.5 per cent (Norway) of girls had done this (Goran Svedin, 2007). In the UK research found 31 per cent of girls and 16 per cent of boys aged 13 to 17 years report having experienced sexual abuse from an intimate partner (Barter *et al.*, 2009).

Sexualization of childhood

In a recent content analysis of computer games, 83 per cent of male characters were portrayed as aggressive, while 60 per cent of female characters were portrayed in a sexualized way and 39 per cent were scantily clad. In the game Rape-Lay, which was available to buy online from Amazon, players take on the role of a rapist who stalks a mother before raping her and her daughters. In Grand Theft Auto players get the chance to beat up prostitutes and in Tour of Duty they can realistically slice to pieces with bullets enemy combatants. While parents have a role in preventing children's access to this technically age-restricted material, the availability of online games on the internet where age is difficult to assess increases the likelihood of children coming into contact with material which is assumed to be only appropriate for adults (Papadopolous, 2009).

⇨

Reflections on the research
Activity 1

Is regulation of commercial interests and access to material on the web the solution to this problem of children and young people being exposed to developmentally inappropriate materials and to the risk of exploitation and abuse by adults?

Activity 2

Should public bodies or adults regulate access or should children to be given the knowledge and skills to protect themselves?

CEOP (Child Exploitation and Online Protection) is a criminal justice organization set up in 2006 that brings together police, social workers and IT experts to protect children and young people from online abuse and exploitation by identifying abusers and abusive materials on the web and taking action against those responsible. CEOP also provides online advice to children and young people, parents and professionals to help them protect themselves/children from online abuse. There are CEOP icons on a growing number of websites that allow internet users to instantly report online abuse. According to CEOP the age of children in abusive images is younger than was previously the case (Hilton, 2011). While police attention has focused on adults who groom and trick young people into producing online abusive images of themselves young people are increasingly involved as image producers.

'Sexting' is a practice which has recently been part of CEOP's child protection work. Sexting involves sending a sexualized image, usually of oneself, to friends or an intimate partner via a mobile phone or other IT. The problem with sexting is that once sent, the young person loses control of the image and it can be passed on and shared and spread across the web, causing the young person upset, embarrassment and exposing her to potential harm and exploitation through other people's use of the image.

Interview with Zoe Hilton about research on sexual exploitation online

Dr Zoe Hilton is head of research at CEOP.
Lorraine Radford: How have the internet and new technologies affected children's vulnerabilities to exploitation and abuse?   ⇨

Interview with Zoe Hilton about research on sexual exploitation online—Cont'd

Zoe Hilton: There is evidence that children are vulnerable in new and challenging environments in the online environment. All children are vulnerable to some degree because they are in a process of development, albeit that there are a range of factors that can make children particularly vulnerable such as having special educational needs or disabilities, growing up in care, having a chaotic family life or experiencing abuse. What appears to occur with the online environment is that it can exacerbate pre-existing vulnerabilities in some children as well as create new potential for vulnerability in others. Some of the online communities, services and spaces appear to deliberately exacerbate children's risk-taking, and many children are introduced to online platforms which are shared spaces with adults they do not know. The availability of web cameras on most new computers means that non-contact forms of abuse are easier, and the opportunities to abuse children are increased.

It is also clear that the online environment has created opportunities for those who wish to abuse and exploit children. Internet forums and websites can provide a virtual community for offenders to chat to one another in order to reinforce distorted thinking about child abuse as well as to share practical advice about how to abuse children. Offenders take advantage of the natural risk-taking and vulnerability of children in online environments and use grooming techniques, posing as boyfriends, celebrities, and school friends to gain access to children.

The internet has created damaging new forms of abuse, in particular non-contact sexual abuse of children via webcam. This is particularly impactful for victims because of the trauma related to feeling complicit in what has occurred as well as the impact of the knowledge of further distribution of abuse material.

Lorraine Radford: What new problems do researchers face in investigating the online exploitation of children?

Zoe Hilton: We already know that children are reluctant to disclose sexual abuse and exploitation, and so any form of research in the area of sexual abuse is likely to be challenging. However, there is evidence to show particular problems with disclosure where children have been victims of images. Researchers and therapists believe that this is because children do not feel in control of the disclosure process. In addition, I think the relatively new nature of online abuse creates both practical and ethical issues because many victims are still children (not ready to disclose what has happened) and therefore it is harder to gain a retrospective ⇨

understanding of the issues from adults. In addition, the recognition and data recording from many agencies around all forms of sexual exploitation needs improving, and online exploitation is often not flagged.

Lorraine Radford: What do you see as the most important gaps in research knowledge about protecting children from harm online?

Zoe Hilton: It would be useful to know more about the impact of the safety messaging and what in particular works, as well as what is effective with different groups of young people. More is also needed about how to reach parents. Research would also be useful on prevention and deterrence with online offenders.

The research referred to previously on the sexualization of childhood was a literature review for the Home Office in 2009 by psychologist Linda Papadopolous. This considered the impact on children's development and learning which exposure to sexualized images has. Papadopolous argued that children have become sexualized in the consumer identity culture of contemporary capitalism. Child sexualization is the imposition of adult sexuality on to children and young people before they are capable of dealing with it, mentally, emotionally or physically.

Sexualization involves the use of sexual attributes as a measure of a person's value and worth and it has four aspects:

1 A person's value comes only from his or her sexual appeal or behaviour, to the exclusion of other characteristics.
2 A person is held to a standard that equates physical attractiveness with being sexy.
3 A person is sexually objectified, made into a thing for others' sexual use, rather than being seen as a person with the capacity for independent action and decision making.
4 Sexuality is inappropriately imposed upon a person.

The internet, video games, clothing, TV, popular music, media and even toys all draw children into the process of sexualization, bombarding them with developmentally inappropriate images, drawing them into sexualized behaviour and interactions, inviting them to rate themselves and others against gender stereotypical sexualized criteria of behaviour and body image.

The sexualization of children pervades many areas of their lives and interactions, especially their leisure time and interaction with peers. Direct marketing of push-up bras for 8-year-olds, pole-dancing kits in toy shops and playboy logos on toddlers' T-shirts, sold to parents as 'cute', push the sexualization of children into the 'normal' areas of everyday life.

Papadopolous argued that the impact on the child will vary with the child's age and development but there is a cumulative impact or 'drip-drip' effect of exposure to violent and sexualized images that, over time, may lead to the normalization of violence against girls and women, cause developmental harm (e.g. as regards the young person's understanding of the role of aggression in intimate relationships), distorted body image, and efforts to present a sexualized image of self that puts the young person at risk (Papadopolous, 2009)

In 2010 the internet-based mothers' group Mumsnet launched a campaign against the sexualization of children called 'Let girls be girls', demanding tighter controls on sexualized products marketed at children. The coalition government appointed Reg Bailey, chief executive of the Mothers' Union, to lead a review in the sexualization of children. The report subsequently recommended greater regulation and more parental control, including:

- new controls upon the internet so that users had to make active choices about whether to allow adult content or not;
- no sexualized imagery to be shown near schools or playgrounds;
- the development of a portal through which parents can lodge complaints about inappropriate materials;
- stronger age ratings for music, videos and stricter TV watersheds;
- regulation to prevent marketing of age-inappropriate clothing for children and young people.

(Bailey, 2011)

Example of research—Sexual victimization of children in the UK

Figure 6.1 shows the rates of reported experiences of sexual abuse in childhood by children and young people from the most recent research into children's and young people's experiences of maltreatment and victimization (see Chapter 1).

Table 6.1 provides the rates for each specific type of contact and non-contact sexual abuse reported by the sample of 2,274 young people aged 11 to 17 years and the sample of 1,761 young adults aged 18 to 24 years reporting on their experiences prior to the age of 18.

⇨

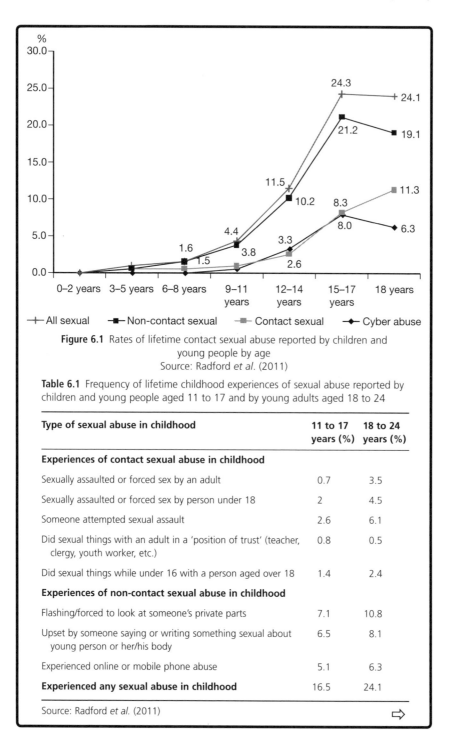

Figure 6.1 Rates of lifetime contact sexual abuse reported by children and young people by age
Source: Radford *et al.* (2011)

Table 6.1 Frequency of lifetime childhood experiences of sexual abuse reported by children and young people aged 11 to 17 and by young adults aged 18 to 24

Type of sexual abuse in childhood	11 to 17 years (%)	18 to 24 years (%)
Experiences of contact sexual abuse in childhood		
Sexually assaulted or forced sex by an adult	0.7	3.5
Sexually assaulted or forced sex by person under 18	2	4.5
Someone attempted sexual assault	2.6	6.1
Did sexual things with an adult in a 'position of trust' (teacher, clergy, youth worker, etc.)	0.8	0.5
Did sexual things while under 16 with a person aged over 18	1.4	2.4
Experiences of non-contact sexual abuse in childhood		
Flashing/forced to look at someone's private parts	7.1	10.8
Upset by someone saying or writing something sexual about young person or her/his body	6.5	8.1
Experienced online or mobile phone abuse	5.1	6.3
Experienced any sexual abuse in childhood	16.5	24.1

Source: Radford *et al.* (2011)

Example of research—Sexual victimization of children in the UK—Cont'd

- The researchers found that young people aged under 18 were the most frequently reported perpetrators of sexual abuse in childhood. Perpetrators were 51 per cent peers, 21.8 per cent adults not living with the child, 20.7 per cent intimate partners, 4.8 per cent parents or guardians, and 3.6 per cent siblings. Persons aged under 18 were 65.9 per cent of the perpetrators reported in the survey (including peers, partners and siblings).
- Girls are the majority of the victims of childhood sexual abuse; 17.8 per cent report a lifetime experience of contact sexual abuse by age 18 compared with 5.1 per cent of boys.
- At ages 12 to 14 the gender difference between male and female rates of reported experiences of contact sexual abuse are smaller; 3 per cent of females have experienced contact sexual abuse by the time they reach 12 to 14 years compared with 2.3 per cent of males.
- By the age of 18 girls have experienced almost double the rates of non-contact sexual abuse compared with boys, The peak ages for reporting a lifetime experience of non-contact sexual abuse were found among young people at ages 15 to 17, when 27.5 per cent of females reported having a lifetime experience of non-contact sexual abuse compared with 15.2 per cent of males (Radford *et al.*, 2011).

Reflections on the research

Activity 1

Consider the data on sexual victimization presented above. What conclusions could you make about the risks of contact and non-contact sexual abuse for children and young people at different ages after age 11?

Activity 2

What conclusions could you make about the risks of online and mobile phone abuse to children of different ages over the age of 11?

The risks of sexual abuse in childhood vary developmentally and by gender with girls aged over 12 being more likely to report contact and non-contact sexual abuse than boys. Childhood sexualization raises questions about children and agency and our traditional approaches to protection, how to balance help to young people with their wishes for autonomy and independence. It is important that steps taken to protect children and young people do not undermine their autonomy and independence, are based on young people's views and experiences, and draw upon available research evidence so that adult fears about risks can be situated alongside research findings.

Summary

- Public policy responses polarize children as either villains or victims so that children and young people who are both victimized and victimizer may have their needs overlooked.
- Media coverage of youth violence generates emotive responses from the general public which have been exploited by politicians and helped to create an increasingly punitive approach to young offenders.
- Balancing the welfare and needs of offenders with justice for victims and public protection is inherently difficult. Mixed objectives in youth justice responses have made it difficult to identify impact and measure outcomes.
- Adult concerns about the commercialization and sexualization of childhood have brought new efforts to regulate. It is important that decisions about improving safety in cyberspace are made in consultation with children and young people, and draw upon research about the risks and impact upon young people's lives.

Further reading

Bailey, R. (2011) *Let Children Be Children*. London: Department for Education.

The review of the sexualization and commercialization of children conducted for the coalition government.

Garrett, P. (2009) *Transforming Children's Services*. Milton Keynes: McGraw Hill/Open University Press, chs 6 and 7.

A thorough and critical review of the Labour government's reforms of children's services including policies on young people and crime.

Papadopolous, L. (2009) *The sexualization of young people review*. London: Home Office

The review of research literature on the impact of the sexualization and commercialization of childhood on children's psychological and emotional well-being and development.

Research details

British Crime Survey

The British Crime Survey is an annual survey of a representative sample of adults and children living in households in England and Wales. About 37,000 adults are interviewed. The survey was extended to cover children aged 10 to 15 in 2009, when 3,661 children and young people were interviewed after their parent had completed the adult survey.

Various publications on the survey are available. For the most recent survey see Chaplin, R., Flatley, J. and Smith, K. (2011) *Crime in England and Wales 2010–11*, London: Home Office (www.homeoffice.gov.uk).

For research on the use of public space by children and young people based on the BCS see Hoare, J., Parfrement-Hopkins, J., Britton, A., Hall, P., Scribbins, M. and Flatley, J. (2011) *Children's Experience and Attitudes Towards the Police, Personal Safety and Public Spaces: Findings from the 2009/10 British Crime Survey Interviews with Children Aged 10 to 15 Supplementary Volume 3 to Crime in England and Wales 2009/10*. London: Home Office.

Playing Outdoors—Play England

A survey of 2,000 parents of children aged between 5 and 16 commissioned from OnePoll in June 2011 by Savlon and Play England.

Further details from www.playday.org.uk.

Sexual victimization in Europe—Goran Svedin (2007)

Part of the Baltic sea study of sexual health involving six nations (Norway, Sweden, Russia, Estonia, Lithuania and Poland) conducting the same survey of 20,000 young persons under the age of 18 to ask them about sexual health and behaviour. The research on selling sex and use of pornography was based on an analysis of findings for 11,528 young people from all the nations included, apart from Russia.

Goran Svedin, C. (2007) 'Experiences with sexual abuse, selling sex and use of pornography', in Mossige, S., Ainsaar, M. and Goran Svedin, C. (eds) *The Baltic Sea Regional Study on Adolescents' Sexuality*. Oslo: NOVA Norwegian Social Research (www.nova.no).

Sexualization of childhood—Papadopolous

Papadopolous reviewed research literature on commercialization and sexualization of childhood for the Home Office in 2009 to 2010.

Papadopolous, L. (2009) *The Sexualization of Young People Review*. London: Home Office.

Sexual victimization of children in the UK

These are findings from the UK-wide study *Child Abuse and Neglect in the UK Today*. This was a household survey of a representative sample of the UK population of families with children and young people aged under 25. The research was conducted for the NSPCC in 2009. Some 6,196 interviews about childhood experiences of maltreatment and victimization were collected from parents reporting for children aged under 11, from children and young people aged 11 to 17 and from young adults aged 18 to 24 using the standard victimization survey methods of Computer Assisted Self Interviewing (CASI), and Audio-CASI (A-CASI), where sensitive questions are asked and answered as privately as possible on a laptop computer, young people hearing questions privately through headphones. Some 2,160 interviews were completed with caregivers of children aged 0 to 10, 2,275 with young people aged 11 to 17 and their primary caregivers, and 1,761 with young adults aged 18 to 24. The research used evaluated measures of victimization and its impact, taking into account the impact on mental health as well as controlling for other experiences of adversity.

For further information see Radford, L., Corral, S., Bradley, C., Fisher, H., Bassett, C., Howat, N. and Collishaw, S. (2011) *Child Abuse and Neglect in the UK Today*. London: NSPCC (www.nspcc.org.uk/childstudy).

Protection, Safeguarding and Prevention

Chapter Outline

Introduction and key questions

Key questions:

- What is being safe?
- What should be the focus of policy and interventions?
- Should policies and interventions identify and target resources at those most at risk of violence or maltreatment?
- Should the focus be on improving child well-being and preventing violence?
- How do we know if children and young people in need of protection are safe from harm?
- How do we know what works?
- Who should be responsible for keeping children and young people safe?

Being safe

What is being safe?

Much of the history of child protection policy in the UK until recently has been about how to deliver services, focusing on the processes of child protection (Department of Health, 1995), rather than on the outcomes and what we mean by being 'safe from harm'. While, as shown in Chapter 1, government guidance has defined different aspects of harm towards children, there have been few attempts to define safety from harm. Safety has been approached as absence of harm, as in identifying and protecting children at risk of significant harm, or in relation to the child's overall health, development or well-being. Children who are maltreated do not always show signs of injury or harm that can be counted as separate incidents. Well-being refers to the quality of the child's life which can be measured objectively, as the absence of violence, poverty, injury, etc., and subjectively, whether or not the child is happy, and feels safe and secure. The advantage of looking at well-being is that children themselves may be asked about how safe they feel.

Under the Children Act 1989, local authorities have responsibilities to safeguard and promote the welfare of children. These include:

- Protecting children from significant harm.
- Preventing impairment of children's health and development.
- Ensuring that children grow up in circumstances consistent with the provision of safe and effective care.
- Undertaking that role so as to enable those children to have optimum life chances to move on to adulthood successfully.

(DCFS, 2010)

The 2004 Children Act placed a statutory duty on agencies to make arrangements to *safeguard and promote the welfare of children*. Safeguarding encompasses child protection (children at risk of significant harm where social workers have a duty to investigate under S47 of the Children Act 1989), taking action where there are concerns about a child in need (under S17 of the Children Act 1989), and safeguarding and promoting the welfare of all children.

Well-being measures are increasingly used in cross-national comparative research to assess children's welfare in different nations. Well-being is typically measured on the basis of how well a child's needs are met, the level of poverty in a society, quality of life, social exclusion and support for children's rights. Thus, well-being is a way to look at being safe, as, in theory, it takes the opposite approach to looking at harm, or at a lack of rights and social exclusions. Well-being measures cover the physical, social and emotional well-being of children in a dynamic way, looking not just at the immediate lives of children but also at their potential to lead fulfilled and happy lives in the future (Statham and Chase, 2010).

Example of research: Child well-being in Europe

Table 7.1 Ranking of 6 out of 20 European nations on child well-being indicators

Country	Average ranking on all 6 indicators	1 Material well-being	2 Health and safety	3 Education	4 Family and peer relations	5 Behaviour and risks	6 Subjective well-being
Netherlands	4.2	10	2	6	3	3	1
Norway	8.7	2	8	11	10	13	8
Italy	10.0	14	5	20	1	10	10
Poland	12.3	21	15	3	14	2	19
Czech Republic	12.5	11	10	9	19	9	17
UK	18.2	18	12	17	21	21	20

Source: UNICEF (2007, p. 2)

Out of 20 European nations, the UK came bottom of the league in the UNICEF report on child well-being in Europe. Comparing the health and safety of children in 25 OECD countries the UK ranked a little better. Twelve countries had above-average overall child health and safety rankings with Sweden at the top (followed by Iceland, the Netherlands, Finland, Denmark, Italy, Spain, France, Norway, Switzerland, the Czech Republic and Germany). The UK was in the bottom 13 nations ranking with below-average health and safety for children at fifteenth, with the USA at the very bottom on this measure. Health and safety was measured by comparing rates of infant death, low birthweight, rates of child immunization and child deaths by accident and injury. Ranking the 25 OECD nations on rates of deaths from accident or injury, Sweden had the lowest rate among the 25 nations and the UK the second lowest. (UNICEF, 2007).

⇨

> **Reflections on the research**
> Activity
>
> What does the UNICEF ranking about child well-being tell you about how well children in these European nations might be protected from harm?

A potential criticism of the UNICEF ranking was that it used data that do not reflect the current experiences of children in the UK. Other research and investigations, including those based on research with young people, has similarly found that children in Britain today have more challenging lives than previously (Layard and Dunn, 2009). Overall child well-being indicators for the UK compare unfavourably with other countries in Western Europe, but the indicators of child maltreatment have been limited to homicide rates, for which the UK is by no means performing the worst (UNICEF, 2003, 2007). This makes it difficult to ascertain the extent to which experiences of maltreatment and victimization or other factors, possibly interlinked, influence poorer health and emotional well-being. As yet, few of the cross-national comparative measures include abuse and victimization of children, mostly because measures do not exist to allow these comparisons to be made, an exception being the Child and Youth Wellbeing Index at Duke University, North Carolina (Land, 2010).

Identification and recognition

Children at risk of significant harm are identified in three ways: (1) when physical or behavioural indicators of abuse or neglect are spotted; (2) when a child tells somebody, or makes a 'disclosure'; (3) when a third party makes a report to a front-line service such as the police or a local authority child protection service.

Indicators of abuse or neglect

Research has shown that there are some common physical and behavioural indicators of abuse. Common potential indicators may include the following.

Injuries

- severe physical injury in an infant or child under the age of 4 in the absence or trauma of medical condition;
- unexplained head injury (subdural haemorrhage) in a child aged under 2;
- fractures in a child under the age of 18 months in the absence of trauma or a medical condition;
- unexplained patterns of bruising or injury with inconsistent explanations; unexplained bruising in babies who are not independently mobile; injuries on soft tissue in concealed areas of the body; injuries showing the mark of an implement;
- adult human bites;
- cigarette burns.

Signs of emotional distress

- panic attacks;
- indicators of disorganised or insecure attachments such as frozen watchfulness.

Developmental indicators

- faltering growth;
- speech delays;
- bed wetting.

Behavioural indicators

- being angry or aggressive;
- stealing or hoarding food;
- sexualized behaviour and age-inappropriate sexual knowledge.

(*Sources*: Gilbert *et al.*, 2008b; Munro, 2007)

Further investigation is needed into physical and behavioural indicators since, although those listed above are highly suggestive of abuse and neglect, some can have alternative explanations. For some children (for example, children living with sexual abuse or with domestic violence), there may not be any signs of physical injury, and behavioural or developmental indicators might have alternative explanations. Talking to the parents or carers and receiving explanations that are inconsistent with the indicators of abuse can help confirm abuse or neglect. The identification of abuse and neglect often requires gathering information from a range of different sources.

Disclosure of abuse

There is a large body of research on abuse disclosure and forensic interviewing with children about experiences of abuse (Bacon and Richardson, 2000; Lamb *et al.*, 2007). The literature shows that many barriers exist to prevent reporting. The age or developmental status of the child and the nature of the relationship with the perpetrator have a profound influence on disclosure (see Chapter 4).

Reports

The third way in which children living with violence, abuse and neglect may be identified is when this is reported to an agency such as the police or children's social care. As shown in Chapter 1, under-reporting for a variety of reasons is known to be an issue. Young people living with maltreatment or victimization and adults who suspect it may be reluctant to report their concerns. Increased reporting can indicate a number of different things including changes in the willingness of individuals to report violence and abuse owing to publicity or changes in policy, an increase in levels of violence and abuse, and increased readiness of children and young people to seek help.

Public inquiries into social work failings and child abuse atrocities have had a strong influence on the development of policy and practice on child protection in England. Two issues have dominated the inquiries: failure to spot and act on maltreatment and misidentification, and acting overzealously. The Children Act 1989 and the Children Act 2004 both followed inquiries prompted by media and public alarm (see Butler-Sloss (1988) for an example of overzealous actions; Laming, (2003) for an example of not acting).

Example of research

Serious case reviews

Brandon *et al.* (2008) studied 161 serious case reviews that occurred between 2003 and 2005. In two-thirds of the cases the children died and one-third were seriously injured. Forty-seven per cent of the children were aged under 1 but

⇨

Example of research—Cont'd

25 per cent were over 11 years old, including 9 per cent who were over 16. Many older children were seen as 'hard to help' as they had experienced long-term maltreatment, were self-harming, substance misusers and often had mental health difficulties. Agencies appeared to have run out of strategies for supporting these older children and were sometimes reluctant to assess the young people as having mental health needs.

Only 12 per cent of the children killed or seriously harmed were on the child protection register but 55 per cent were known to children's social care services at the time of the incident. The families where children were physically injured were in contact with universal and adult services rather than with children's social care. In families where children suffered from long-term neglect, children's social care often failed to take into account the past history and adopted an optimistic 'start again syndrome' which involved putting aside the previous history. Where information was available on circumstances it was found that well over half of the children had been living with domestic violence, or parental mental ill-health, or parental substance misuse. These problems often co-existed.

Problems with identification and gaining information about the abuse or neglect found by the researchers included:

- Parents were often hostile towards helping agencies and workers were frightened to visit the family home.
- Apparent or disguised cooperation by parents often hindered awareness of the abuse.
- Parents made it difficult for professionals to see the children.
- Reluctant family engagement coupled with frequent house moves made records sketchy.
- Problems of communication and information sharing between agencies meant that only partial pictures of the family history emerged.

(Brandon *et al.*, 2008)

Reflections on the research

What strategies would be needed to overcome some of the barriers to identification and response highlighted by this research?

On the opposite side to not identifying sits the problem of 'inappropriate' referrals discussed in the Munro review of child protection, where it is thought that children are referred when they are not in need of additional help (Munro, 2010). Contact with children's social care that later proves to have been unnecessary has consequences for a family who have to live with the views of others that 'there is no smoke without fire'. A large number of referrals can be a problem if there are insufficient resources to deal with them. In 2005 S120 of the Adoption and Children Act 2002 implemented the principle that children who see or overhear violence towards another person in the home can be at risk of suffering significant harm. This brought a huge increase in police notifications to children's social care, and in some cases services were overwhelmed and struggling to find solutions about how to cope and how to identify those in need of a fast response (Stanley *et al.*, 2010). Referrals on the basis of emotional abuse increased at this time (Figure 7.1), and it is highly likely that referrals were influenced by this emphasis on children living with domestic violence. Subsequently there were also huge increases of referrals brought by the publicity over the death of baby Peter Connelly (see Chapter 1).

In contrast to media constructions of child abuse or neglect, it is uncertainty and complexity which is a key feature in cases where children are in need of protection (Munro, 2010). Responsibilities are shared across a range of different services for adults and children. Information sharing and

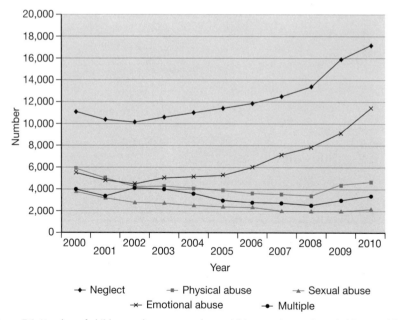

Figure 7.1 Number of children and young people on child protection registers/subject to child protection plans at 31 March 2000 to 2010, by category of abuse (England)
Source: Department of Education (2010)

communication between services can be poor to non-existent. Children's needs vary. There are inherent tensions in social work where social workers are expected to work in partnership with parents, to support and help families with problems, as well as exert control and step in as agents of the state to protect children from harm. Research shows that parents and children can have feelings of fear and stigma about involvement with social workers (Corby, 2006).

Different approaches to being safe

- What should be the focus of policy and interventions?
- Should policies and interventions identify and target resources at those most at risk of violence or maltreatment?
- Should the focus be on improving child well-being and preventing violence?

The history of child protection policy in England shows that these tensions associated with protecting children resurface periodically (Corby, 2006; Parton, 1985, 2006). There have been major changes in the approach to child protection in England in recent years, broadening the focus from child protection, to safeguarding and promoting child welfare and to providing a 'good life' for children (Gilbert *et al.*, 2011). Table 7.2 illustrates some key differences in approach. The first three columns in table 7.2 summarize the key features of child protection policy in England from the early 1990s to 2010. Column 4 presents core features of the public health prevention approach discussed in Chapter 3. The coalition government have promoted the idea of greater emphasis on prevention (Allen, 2011). Column 5 sets out features of a children's rights approach (key provisions featured in table 7.3).

In the 1990s, child protection in England was viewed as operating like a big sieve, assessing referrals to local authority services to determine if children met the thresholds for rationed social work intervention (Corby, 2006). Preoccupation with thresholds was procedural, legalistic and risk averse, and is generally recognized as being influenced by the concerns about too much child protection intervention into families engendered by paediatricians' and social workers' actions examined in the Cleveland child sexual abuse inquiry (Fox-Harding,1996). The Children Act 1989 aimed partly to improve working together across different agencies, strengthen the principle of partnership working with parents and put more responsibility on to parents.

Table 7.2 Different approaches to child protection and safeguarding

	Child Protection	Target vulnerable children	Safeguard and promote child welfare	Prevention	Child's right
Children included	Children at risk of significant harm	Children at risk of significant harm Children in need	All children	All children	All children
Core focus of activities	Identify those who meet thresholds Evidence of risk	Framework of assessment of children in need	Achieving five outcomes—be healthy, be safe, achieve full potential, contribute to community	Prevention of harm occurring or recurring, harm reduction	Right to life Protection Provision Overcome harm Prevention Participation Non-discrimination
Mechanisms	Court ordered child protection plan Working together	Targeted family support for vulnerable Working together	'Progressive universalism' Continuum of needs Integrated system Centrally driven planning, target setting and performance monitoring	Reducing risks Increasing protective factors	Implementation of child's rights
Allocation of services	Service follows verification of risk of harm	Early intervention to children in need	Early intervention to vulnerable Sure Start Social exclusion	Prevention Evidence-based early intervention	State-determined
Rights and responsibilities	Family vs. state	Family supported	State encourages parental responsibilities	Community responsibilities	Global/national responsibilities
Policy example	Early days of Children Act 1989	Messages from Research DoH (1995)	Children Act 2004	World Health Organization Butchart et al. (2006)	International child sex tourism

Table 7.3 United Nations Convention on the Rights of the Child articles relevant to being safe

Category of Rights	Article	Description of right
Protection	6	Inherent right to life, state responsibilities to ensure survival and development
	19	State obligations to protect children from all forms of maltreatment by parents or others responsible for their care and to undertake preventive and treatment programmes in this regard
	34	Protection from sexual exploitation and abuse, including prostitution and involvement in pornography
	37	No child to be subject to torture, cruel treatment or punishment, life imprisonment, unlawful arrest or deprivation of liberty; this includes restrictions of liberty for 'welfare' purposes as well as penal
Provision	20	Obligations to provide special protection to children deprived of their family environment and ensure that alternative family or institutional care is made available, taking into account child's cultural background
Overcoming harm	39	Child victims of armed conflict, torture, neglect, maltreatment or exploitation to receive appropriate treatment for their recovery and reintegration
Prevention	35	Prevention of sale of child, child trafficking and abduction
Non-discrimination	2	Rights apply to all children irrespective of race, colour, sex, language, religion, political or other opinion, national ethnic or social origin, disability, birth or other status
Participation	12	The child's right to express an opinion, to have that opinion taken into account in any matter or procedure affecting the child

Examples from research: Messages from research

The Department of Health published *Messages from Research* in 1995. This identified a number of problems with an investigative child protection approach

- Although acts of serious physical violence and sexual abuse occur, harm to children rarely results from a one-off incident of abuse. It is living in an abusive environment over time that has harmful consequences.
- Emotional neglect greatly influences poor outcomes but the focus on child protection poorly addressed this problem.
- There was too much emphasis on investigation and forensic proof of significant harm, and too little attention given to welfare, prevention and treatment.
- An adversarial legalistic focus on 'proof' of abuse or neglect can be detrimental to children's well-being, since expert testimony is often divided and evidence uncertain.

⇨

- Children in need were filtered out of the system and received no support, or support that was discretionary.
- Thresholds vary and may be based more on resources available than on levels of need.
- Families are often resentful and avoidant of child protection involvement which is widely seen to be coercive and causing stigma rather than supportive.
- There was little evidence of engaging with parents and working in partnership with parents.

(Department of Health, 1995)

Reflections on the research

What might be the possible solutions to these difficulties? Consider the pros and cons of the following options:

- surveillance of the child's well-being;
- providing services to those who do not meet the child protection threshold;
- programmes to improve parenting;
- deciding cases out of court;
- more precise, research-based risk assessment to determine risk of harm;
- better assessment of the child's overall welfare needs in context;
- befriending and home visiting for vulnerable families;
- advocacy for children.

Messages from Research prompted a re-focusing towards earlier intervention and providing appropriate services for children on the basis of *need* rather than whether or not the child protection threshold was met (Department of Health, 1995). In 2000 the Department of Health introduced an Assessment Framework for Children in Need, which took an ecological approach to assessment of the child's needs at the individual, family and environmental levels (Figure 7.2).

Factors to be assessed along each of the ecological levels are shown on each side of the triangle of the assessment framework diagram and help identify the range of needs and services required for the child's package of care.

Under the Labour government the emphasis moved towards universally promoting child welfare and intervening with vulnerable children and families to deal with social exclusion. A radical change came with the Children Act 2004 which shifted the focus from the processes of child

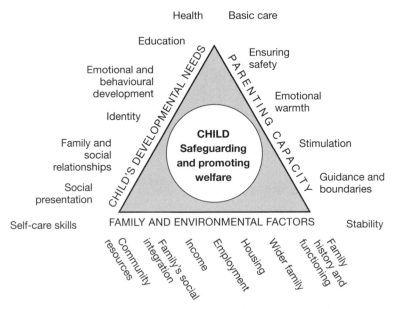

Figure 7.2 The assessment framework for children in need
Source: Department of Health (2000)

protection investigation to 'safeguarding' and promoting child welfare to meet the five outcomes for all children set out in the *Every Child Matters* Green Paper (HM Government, 2003). The five outcomes for all children were: being healthy; staying safe; enjoyment of school and educational achievement; making positive contributions to their communities; and achieving economic well being. Clearly the promotion of welfare to meet these five outcomes requires a broader range of activities than ensuring the absence of harm.

The new focus on outcomes for all children was accompanied by a variation on targeting, 'progressive universalism', to meet the needs of those who were vulnerable to social exclusion. This involved:

- a much greater emphasis on the early identification of need;
- providing a range of early intervention and family support services (including extended schools, Sure Start children's centres, FIPs, etc.);
- national targets and performance monitoring of compliance;
- integrated information systems and data sharing;
- improving working together across a range of different local services, including appointments of lead professionals for children with complex needs to coordinate services across a number of different agencies;
- the introduction of the common assessment framework (CAF).

The CAF was to be an easy-to-use practical tool for any professional who felt that the child might not reach one or more of the five *Every Child Matters* outcomes without additional services.

The movement to broaden safeguarding further to become everyone's responsibility was made by the previous government's *Staying Safe Action Plan* (HM Government, 2008), based on the first ten-year plan for children, (HM Government, 2007). These documents set out detailed plans for improving child safety and the range of services needed from universal services (for all children), to targeted services (for those who are at greater risk) to responsive services (for those in need of protection and help to overcome the harm of abuse) (HM Government, 2008, p. 7). Ideally, the vision was that services would be appropriate to meet the continuum of needs of children across these different levels with parenting (in practice mostly by mothers), very much a key feature in meeting children's needs (Figure 7.3).

Control and target-driven monitoring was a defining feature of the previous Labour government's approach to public services. A set of national targets was developed to allow measurement of progress to meet the five *Every Child Matters* outcomes, with defined indicators and processes for inspection and

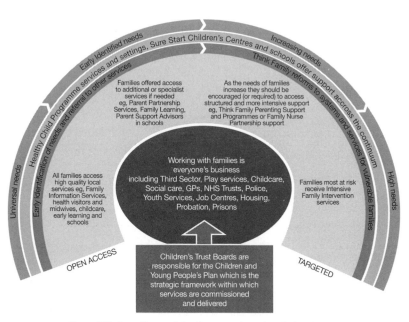

Figure 7.3 Parenting and family support services in local areas
Source: DCSF (2010b)

monitoring. Guidance on *Working Together* (DCSF, 2010a) and a range of tool kits were produced. There were concerns that there was too much guidance and too many targets and measures, creating a bureaucratic burden on professionals and taking their attention away from their everyday work with families (Mesie *et al.*, 2007). Targets could foster perverse incentives, professionals meeting the target even where this may not be the best option for an individual child. Professional discretion and competence were undermined (Munro, 2010). The Munro review of child protection concluded that efforts to improve practice had actually made things worse (Munro, 2011b).

The coalition government wanted a stronger focus on prevention, on giving early help and a freeing of social workers and local authorities from bureaucracy. Locally defined priorities and decision-making were favoured in the policy of 'localism' (HM Government, 2011a, 2011b). Munro (2007) had previously summed up the map of services needed to make children safe as:

- preventing abuse and neglect from occurring;
- preventing low-level problems from getting worse,
- preventing child abuse and neglect from recurring;
- preventing abuse and neglect from causing long-term harm by giving therapeutic support.

In the future, needs and priorities were to be determined at the local levels, supported by central government providing the tools and knowledge about effective approaches to prevention to guide local developments. New health and well-being boards were to be established to bring together health, children's services and community safety and crime control agencies to jointly plan services to meet needs.

The new approach would be one that:

- *Valued professional expertise* by reducing regulation, rules and procedures; promoting 'intelligent' and locally interrogated use of performance monitoring to create an approach that was timely, effective and promoted learning about next steps; and creating a new unannounced inspection framework that put experiences of children and their families at the heart of the system. The new inspection system was to look at the role of all agencies involved with children.
- *Shared responsibility for the provision of early help* to create transparent arrangements for determining local levels of need, the range of services to meet those needs, and mechanisms to identify children requiring referral for social care or protection. Sure Start centres and an expansion in numbers of

health visitors were to be a key resource for earlier identification. Community budgets were set up to enable local authorities to access evidence-based intensive and coordinated interventions for families, including FIPs.
- *Developed social work expertise and supported effective social work practice.*
- *Strengthened accountabilities and promoted learning,* reflecting critically on practice to identify problems and opportunities for improvement. (HM Government, 2011a)

Activity

- Is it possible to improve children's safety and welfare in the context of doing 'more for less'?
- How do you think localism might effect public attitudes towards local authority roles in child protection?

How do we know what works?

How do we know if children and young people in need of protection are safe from harm?

Children's services have been subject to an unprecedented level of evaluation and evidence gathering to identify what is effective. There now exist a number of well-researched approaches for working with vulnerable families shown to reduce risks of poor outcomes for children, home visiting programmes and family nurse partnerships being the best known (e.g. Olds *et al.*, 1997). Although a lot of the original research has been initiated overseas, mostly in the USA, evidence is growing from evaluations in the UK (Allen, 2011). Sure Start was extensively evaluated and over 60 research reports are currently available on various aspects of the programme. Early evaluations showed that the most vulnerable families were not being targeted and Sure Start workers lacked awareness of child protection (Tunstill and Allnock, 2007). By the time of the final evaluation, Sure Start had changed its approach with greater use of outreach for the more excluded and it was recognized as successful in meeting the needs of socially excluded families (HM Government, 2011a; Melhuish *et al.*, 2008).

Spending in the UK on family welfare between 1980 and 2005 was the highest among a group of ten nations studied in a comparative study, and a merging of previously very different approaches was observed. Approaches to child welfare in nations such as Sweden, previously regarded as being more favourable, were much closer to that demonstrated in the UK and it could be said that a children's rights approach was in development in several European nations (Gilbert *et al.*, 2011). As yet there are no available indicators to show the extent of this improvement for children's safety and overall well-being in the UK compared with other European nations. Despite the investment in Sure Start, outcomes for the health of children showed only modest change and in some areas have worsened (Audit Commission, 2010).

For the coalition, target compliance was to be swapped for incentives to produce services that could demonstrate value for money and effectiveness via research evidence and social impact. Creating incentives with a focus on value for money, joint commissioning and 'social impact bonds', where the public sector only pays for positive outcomes, were key features of a new approach to commissioning for the voluntary sector. Radical changes to commissioning frameworks were initiated for health, social care and crime prevention to shift the balance of decision-making to the local level, with greater involvement and participation of individuals in the community and encouraging payment by results. Sure Start children's centres were to focus more upon vulnerable children, being rewarded via payment by results, so that those engaging successfully through outreach with disadvantaged families could be rewarded through the payment system (Hansard, 2011). Participatory budgeting would bring accountability to the local community, potentially offering a way forward on the reality gap between what official statistics show and what the general population thinks. The proposed inclusion of children in determining needs and services could potentially open the door to a radical rethinking of safeguarding.

Rethinking safety

Who should be responsible for keeping children and young people safe? What should be the balance of responsibilities between families, the community and the state?

Khyra Ishaq

Khyra Ishaq starved to death in her home in Birmingham in 2008. Her three brothers aged 12, 9 and 8 and two sisters aged 11 and 4 were also found to be emaciated and taken to hospital. Khyra and her siblings had been taken out

⇨

of school earlier that year after being bullied. Social workers were alerted to the alleged problems in the family a year before Khyra died. An education welfare officer had notified social services several weeks before the child died because she had no reply when she knocked on the door of the house. Neighbours said that Khyra had been so hungry during the last few weeks of her life that she had stolen bread from a bird table.

(*Daily Mail*, 26 May 2008)

Activity

Who out of the following were responsible for Khyra's safety?

- Her parents
- Other children
- Neighbours
- People in the community
- School
- Professionals.

Most policy debates on child protection focus on the responsibilities of professionals or parents, although, as previously argued, children and young people turn to friends or people they know for support first. Previously, government policy has referred to 'safeguarding as everybody's responsibility' and now building trust in communities, but what does this actually mean in practice?

Example of research—Strong Communities

In North West Carolina a community is five years through a ten-year programme to build systems of social support for families to prevent child maltreatment and create a safe community. The programme includes a wide range of community organizations including schools, churches, health centres, civic groups, parent groups as well as individuals who act as volunteers. The community outreach workers recruit citizens and institutions and mobilise volunteers. Young families enroll in strong communities mostly through health services and are given information and support especially during the early years of parenting. Early results show that individuals, parents and organizations can be successfully mobilized to take part but as yet it is too soon to show findings of the impact on outcomes.

(Kimborough-Melton and Campbell, 2008)

Reflections on the research
Activity

Consider the challenges and opportunities for developing social capital in communities so that young people and adults feel responsibility for creating a safe community.

Summary

- Much of the recent history of child protection has focused on delivering services rather than on what it means for children to be safe. Child well-being measures provide an opportunity to look at being safe from a child's point of view.
- Maltreatment can be identified from physical, developmental or behavioural indicators, a child's disclosure or a report made to an agency such as the police or children's social care. A number of barriers operate against identification including poor recognition and information sharing between agencies that are collectively responsible for providing services.
- In contrast to media and campaigning messages about children and violence it is the complexity and uncertainty of working with maltreatment that has been a major area of concern for social work. Problems with under-recognition and misdiagnosis have been regular features of child protection enquiries.
- The focus of children's policy in England has expanded from protecting children from harm to include safeguarding and promoting welfare, to tackling social exclusion, prevention and ensuring that children have a 'good childhood'.
- Cross-national research shows a convergence in approaches to children's welfare policies across Europe and a stronger emphasis than before on promoting children's rights.
- Measuring the impact of policy on children's safety from harm is difficult and the focus has been mostly on quantitative measures and performance monitoring. Despite good intentions these seem to have had a detrimental effect on practice.
- Recent policy provides an opportunity for a much greater level of participation by children and young people themselves in defining needs and having a say in services.
- There is scope to build on learning about what needs to be done to work with children and young people to build social support, social capital and to create the conditions and relationships that foster trusting and safe communities.

Further reading

Gilbert, N., Parton, N. and Skivenes, M. (eds) (2011)
Child Protection Systems International Trends and Orientations. Oxford: Oxford University Press.

A cross-national comparative study of child protection responses in Europe looking at changes in the past 15 years.

Munro, E. (2011) *The Munro Review of Child Protection Final Report: A Child Centered System*. London: Department for Education (available online at http://www.education.gov.uk/munroreview/).

The only review of child protection not to be done in response to a crisis commissioned by the coalition government.

Research details

Child well-being in Europe—UNICEF (2007)

The research was based on official data on child well-being in 20 European countries and 25 OECD nations. The data were ranked and an overall score on six areas was created.

UNICEF (2007) *Child Poverty in Perspective: An Overview of Child Wellbeing in Rich Countries*. Florence: Innocenti Research Centre (www.unicef-icdc. org).

Serious case reviews—Brandon *et al.*, (2008)

One hundred and sixty-one serious case reviews for 2003 to 2005 were analysed (47 in depth) to identify common factors and lessons for practice.

Brandon, M., Belderson, P., Warren, C., Howe, D., Gardner, R., Dodsworth, J. and Black, J. (2008) *Analysing Child Deaths and Serious Injury Through Abuse and Neglect: What can we Learn? A Biennial Analysis of Serious Case Reviews 2003–2005*. London: Department for Children, Schools and Families.

Messages from research (1995)

This was a series of research projects commissioned by the Department of Health on child protection.

Department of Health (1995) *Child Protection Messages from Research*. London: Department of Health.

Strong communities

This is a ten-year programme of research in South Carolina designed to build a whole community system of social support using community organizers to mobilize. The research will measure outcomes in the future.

Kimborough-Melton, R. and Campbell, R. (2008) 'Strong communities for children: A community wide approach to prevention of child abuse and neglect'. *Family and Community Health*, 31(2): 100–112.

References and Further Reading

Action For Children (2009) Neglect campaign advertisement (*www.actionforchildren.org.uk*).

Ainsworth, M., Blehar, M., Waters, E. and Wall, S. (1978) *Patterns of Attachment: A Psychological Study of the Strange Situation*. Hilldale, NJ: Lawrence Erbaum.

Alaggia, R. (2004) 'Many ways of telling: Expanding conceptualizations of child sexual abuse disclosure', *Child Abuse and Neglect*, 28: 1213–1227.

Allen, G. (2011) *Early Intervention: The Next Steps. An Independent Report to Her Majesty's Government*. London: The Cabinet Office.

Armstrong, L. (1978) *Kiss Daddy Goodnight*. New York: Hawthorn

Arnull, E. and Eagle, S. (2009) *Girls and Offending—Patterns, Perceptions and Interventions*. London: Youth Justice Board.

Antropus, S. (2009) *Dying to belong: An In Depth Review of Street Gangs in Britain*. London: Centre for Social Justice.

Arseneault, L., Walsh, E. *et al.* (2006) 'Bullying victimization uniquely contributes to adjustment problems in young children: A nationally representative cohort study.' *Pediatrics*, 118(1): 130–138.

Audit Commission (2010) *Giving Children a Healthy Start: Health Report*. London: Audit Commission.

Bacon, H. and Richardson, S. (2000) 'Child sexual abuse and the continuum of victim disclosure', in Itzin, C. (ed.) *Home Truths about Child Sexual Abuse*. London: Routledge (pp. 235–276).

Bailey, R. (2011) *Letting Children Be Children*. London: Department for Education (www.dfe.gov.uk).

Bandura, A.(1973) *Aggression A Social Learning Analysis*. Princeton, NJ: Prentice Hall.

Barlow, J. and Schrader-McMillan, A. (2010) *Safeguarding Children from Emotional Maltreatment*. London: Jessica Kingsley.

Barter, C. and Berridge, D. (2010) *Children Behaving Badly: Peer Violence between Children and Young People*. London: Wiley.

Barter, C., McCarry, M., Berridge, D. and Evans, K. (2009) *Partner Exploitation and Violence in Teenage Intimate Relationships*. London: NSPCC (www.nspcc.org.uk/Inform).

Belsky, J. (1980) 'Child maltreatment: An ecological integration.' *American Psychologist*, 35(4): 320–335.

Belsky, J. (1993) 'Etiology of child maltreatment: A developmental-ecological analysis.' *Psychological Bulletin*, 114(3): 413–434.

Bentovim, A., Cox, A., Bingley Miller, L. and Pizzey, S. (2009) *Safeguarding Children Living with Trauma and Family Violence: Evidence Based Assessment, Analysis and Planning Interventions*. London: Jessica Kingsley.

Bolt, C. (1993) *The Women's Movement in the United States and Britain from the 1790s to the 1920s.* London: Harvester/Wheatsheaf.

Bowlby, J. (1988) *A Secure Base.* London: Routledge.

Brandon, M., Belderson, P., Warren, C., Howe, D., Gardner, R., Dodsworth, J. and Black, J. (2008) *Analysing Child Deaths and Serious Injury Through Abuse and Neglect: What can we Learn? A Biennial Analysis of Serious Case Reviews 2003-2005.* London: Department for Children, Schools and Families.

Bronfenbrenner, U. (1977) 'Toward an experimental ecology of human development.' *American Psychologist,* July: 513–551.

Bronfenbrenner, U. (1986) 'Ecology of the family as a context for human development: Research perspectives.' *Developmental Psychology,* 22(6): 723–742.

Brookes, M., Lanley, T. and Paterson, K. (2010) *Scaling Up For the Big Society.* London: New Philanthropy Capital (www.philanthropycapital.org).

Browne, A. and Finkelhor, D. (1985) 'The traumatic impact of child sexual abuse: A conceptualization.' *American Journal of Orthopsychiatry,* 55(4): 530–541.

Budd, T., Sharp, C., Weir, G., Wilson, D. and Owen, N. (2005) *Young People and Crime: Findings from the 2004 Offending, Crime and Justice Survey.* London: Home Office (www.homeoffice.gov.uk).

Burton, D., Duty, K. and Leibowitz, G. (2011) 'Differences between sexually victimized and nonsexually victimized male adolescent sexual abusers: Developmental antecedents and behavioral comparisons.' *Journal of Child Sexual Abuse,* 20(1): 77–93.

Butchart, A., Putney, H., Furniss, T. and Kahane, T. (2006) *Preventing Child Maltreatment: a Guide to Taking Action and Generating Evidence.* Geneva: World Health Organization.

Butler-Sloss, E. (1988) *Report of the Inquiry into Child Abuse in Cleveland.* London: HMSO.

Campbell, B. (1988) *Unofficial Secrets: Child Sexual Abuse: The Cleveland Case.* London: Virago.

Carlen, P. (1988) *Women, Crime and Poverty.* Milton Keynes: Open University Press.

Carrabine, E., Iganski, P. *et al.* (2004). *Criminology: A Sociological Introduction.* London: Routledge.

Chaplin, R., Flatley, J. and Smith, K. (2011) *Crime in England and Wales 2010-11.* London: Home Office (www.homeoffice.gov.uk).

ChildLine (2009) *Children Talking to ChildLine About Suicide: Casenotes.* London: NSPCC (www.nspcc.org.uk).

ChildLine (2011) *Data on Counselling Calls 2005-2011.* London: ChildLine.

Chitsabesan, P., Kroll, L., Bailey, S., Kenny, C., MacDonald, W. and Theodosiou, L. (2006) 'Mental health and the needs of young offenders in custody and in the community.' *British Journal of Psychiatry,* 188: 534–540.

Cloward, R. and Ohlin, L. (1960) *Delinquency and Opportunity.* London: Macmillan.

Cobbe, F. P. (1878) 'Wife torture in England.' *Contemporary Review,* April extracts republished in Radford, J. and Russell, D. (eds) (1992) *Femicide: The Politics of Woman Killing.* Milton Keynes: Open University Press (pp. 46–52).

Cohen, A .(1955) *Delinquent Boys.* New York: Free Press.

Corby, B. (2006) *Child Abuse: Towards a Knowledge Base.* Milton Keynes: Open University Press.

Cossar, A., Brandon, M. and Jordan, P. (2011) *Don't Make Assumptions; Children and Young People's*

Views of the Child Protection System and Messages for Change. London: Office of the Children's Commissioner (www.childrenscommissioner.gov.uk).

Cunningham, H. (2006) *The Invention of Childhood*. London: BBC Books.

Daily Mail (2008) 'Half of British adults are scared of children who "behave like feral animals"'. Laura Clark (*http://www.dailymail.co.uk/news/article-1086466/Half-British-adults-scared-children-behave-like-feral-animals.html#ixzz1G7XhH29Q*).

Daily Mail (2010) 'Social services' betrayal let girl, 7, starve to death in modern Britain with a full fridge in the kitchen: nine officials who could have saved Khyra'. Fay Schlesiner, David Wilkes and Andy Dolan, 26 February.

Daily Mail (2011) 'Beaten to death' (*http://www.dailymail.co.uk/news/article-2007302/Ryan-Lovell-Hancox-Toddler-died-hands-carers-despite-killers-known-authorities.html#ixzz1Ro8r0ueJ*).

DEMOS (2007) *Seen and Heard Reclaiming the Public Realm with Children and Young People*. London: DEMOS/Play England.

Department of Education (2010) *Children in Need in England Including Their Characteristics and Further Information on Children Who Were the Subject of a Child Protection Plan 2009–2010*. Statistical release (available at www.education.gov.uk/rsgateway/DB/STR/d000970/index.shtml).

DCSF (2008) *Staying Safe Action Plan*. London: DCSF (www.dcsf.gov.uk).

DCSF (2009) *Youth Crime: Young People Aged 10–17 Receiving Their First Reprimand, Warning or Conviction, in England, 2000–01 to 2008–9*. Statistical release London: DCSF.

DCSF (2010a) *Working Together to Safeguard Children* (3rd edn). London: DCSF (www.dcfs.org.uk).

DCSF (2010b) *Parenting and Family Support Guidance for Local Authorities*. London: DCSF.

Department of Health (1995) *Child Protection Messages from Research*. London: Department of Health.

Department of Health (1999) *Working Together to Safeguard Children: A Guide to Inter-Agency Working to Safeguard and Promote the Welfare of Children*. London: Department of Health.

Department of Health, Department for Education and Employment, and Home Office (2000) *Framework for the Assessment of Children in Need and their Families*. London: The Stationery Office.

Dobash, R. and Dobash, R. (1978) *Violence Against Wives: A Case Against the Patriarchy*. Sussex: Open Books.

Donzelot, J. (1980) *The Policing of Families*. London: Hutchinson.

Downes, D. (2010) 'Counterblast: What went right? New Labour and crime control.' *The Howard Journal*, 49(4): 394–397.

Droisen, E. and Driver, E. (eds) (1989) *Child Sexual Abuse: Feminist Perspectives*. London: Macmillan.

Duffy, B., Wake, W., Burrows, T. and Bremmer, P. (2008) *Closing the Gaps: Crime and Public Perceptions*. IPSO MORI.

Edwards, S. (1989) *Policing Domestic Violence*. London: Sage.

Eisner, M. and Ribeaud, D. (2010) 'Risk factors for aggression in pre-adolescence: risk domains, cumulative risk and gender differences: results from a prospective longitudinal study of a multi ethnic urban sample'. *European Journal of Criminlogy*, 11: 460–498.

Emsley, C. (2005) *Crime and Society 1750–1900* (3rd edn). London: Pearson/Longman.

Evening Standard (2011) '"Unstable" mother let baby starve to death' (9 March).

Farmer, E. and Lutman, E. (2009) *Case Management and Outcomes for Neglected Children Returned to their Parents: A Five Year Follow-up Study*. Report to the Department for Children, Schools and Families, School for Policy Studies, University of Bristol.

Farmer, E., Sturgess, W. and O'Neill, T. (2008) *The Reunification of Looked After Children With Their Parents: Patterns Interventions and Outcomes*. Report to the Department for Children, Schools and Families, School for Policy Studies, University of Bristol.

Farrall, S., Bottoms, A. and Shapland, J. (2010) 'Social structures and desistance from crime.' *European Journal of Criminology*, 7(6): 546–570.

Farrington, D. and Painter, K. (2004) *Gender Differences in Offending: Implications for Risk Focused Prevention*. Home Office Online Report 09/04. London: Home Office (www.homeoffice.gov.uk).

Farrington, D., Coid, J., Harnett, L., Joliffe, D., Soteriou, N., Turner, R. and West, D. (2006) *Criminal Careers up to Age 50 and Life Success Up to Age 48: New Findings from the Cambridge Study in Delinquent Development*. London: Home Office (www.homeoffice.gov.uk).

Featherstone, B., Hooper, C., Scourfield, J. and Taylor, J. (eds) (2010) *Gender and Child Welfare in Society*. Chichester: Wiley-Blackwell.

Finkelhor, D. (2007) 'Developmental victimology: The comprehensive study of childhood victimizations, in Davis, A. and Herman, S. *Victims of Crime*. Thousand Oaks, CA: Sage: (pp. 9–34).

Finkelhor, D. (2008) *Childhood Victimization*. Oxford: Oxford University Press.

Finklehor, D. and Jones, L. (2006) 'Why have child maltreatment and child victimization declined?' *Journal of Social Issues*, 62(4): 685–716.

Finkelhor, D., Ormrod, R. and Turner, H. (2005a)'Re-victimization patterns in a national longitudinal sample of children and youth.' *Child Abuse and Neglect*, 31: 479–502.

Finkelhor, D., Ormrod, R. K. and Turner, H. A. (2006) 'Kid's stuff: The nature and impact of peer and sibling violence in younger and older children'. *Child Abuse and Neglect*, 30(1): 401–442.

Finkelhor, D., Ormrod, R. K. and Turner, H. A. (2009) 'Lifetime assessment of poly-victimization in a national sample of children and youth.' *Child Abuse and Neglect*, 33(7): 403–411.

Finkelhor, D., Ormrod, D., Turner, H. A. and Hamby, S. (2005b) Measuring polyvictimization using the Juvenile Victimization Questionnaire.' *Child Abuse and Neglect*, 29: 1297–1312.

Finkelhor, D., Turner, H., Ormrod, R. and Hamby, S. (2010) 'Trends in childhood violence and abuse exposure: evidence from two national surveys.' *Archives in Pediatric and Adolescent Medicine*, 164(3): 238–242.

Fitzgerald, M., Stockdale, J. and Hale, C. (2003) *Young People and Street Crime*. London: Youth Justice Board.

Flatley, J., Kershaw, C., Smith, K., Chaplin, R. and Moon, D. (eds) (2010) *Crime in England and Wales 2009/10: Findings from the British Crime Survey and Police recorded crime* (3rd edn). London: Home Office (http://www.homeoffice.gov.uk/rds/index.html).

Fonagy, P., Target, M., Cottrell, D., Phillips, J. and Kurtz, Z. (2002) *What Works For Whom? A Critical Review of Treatments for Children and Adolescents*. London: Guilford Press.

Fox-Harding, L. (1996) *Family, State and Social Policy*. London: Macmillan.

Fraser, D. (1973) *The Evolution of the British Welfare State*. London: Macmillan.

Frean, A. (2008) 'Most adults think children "are feral and a danger to society"'. *The Times*, 17 November.

Freisthler, B., Morritt, D. and Lescala, E. (2006) 'Understanding the ecology of child maltreatment: A review of the literature and directions for further research.' *Child Maltreatment*, 11(3): 263–280.

Frost, N. and Parton, N. (2009) *Understanding Children's Social Care*. London: Sage.

Furedi, F. and Bristow, J. (2008) *Licensed to Hug*. London: Civitas.

Garland, D. (2001) *The Culture of Control*. Oxford: Oxford University Press.

Gelles, R. and Straus, M. (1988) *Intimate Violence*. New York: Simon & Schuster.

Gilbert, N . (2004). *Transformation of the Welfare State: The Silent Surrender of Public Responsibility*. New York: Oxford University Press.

Gilbert, N., Parton, N. and Skivenes, M, (eds) (2011) *Child Protection Systems: International Trends and Orientations*. Oxford: Oxford University Press

Gilbert, R., Spatz Widom, C., Browne, K., Fergusson, D., Webb, E. and Janson, S. (2008a) 'Burden and consequences of child maltreatment in high-income countries.' *The Lancet*, December: 720 (www. thelancet.com).

Gilbert, R., Kemp, A., Thoburn, J., Sidebotham, P., Radford, L., Glaser, D. and Macmillan, H. (2008b) 'Recognizing and responding to child maltreatment.' *The Lancet,* December: 21–34.(www. thelancet.com).

Global Initiative to End all Corporal Punishment of Children (2010) *Global Progress Towards Prohibiting All Corporal Punishment* (December) (www.endcorporalpunishment.org).

Glueck, S. and Glueck, E. (1950) *Unravelling Juvenile Delinquency*. New York: Commonwealth Fund.

Goldson, H. (2002) 'Children, crime and the state', in Goldson, B., Lavalette, M. and McKechnie, J. (eds) *Children. Welfare and the State*. London: Sage (pp. 120–135).

Goran Svedin, C. (2007) 'Experiences with sexual abuse, selling sex and use of pornography', in Mossige, S., Ainsaar, M. and Goran Svedin, C. (eds) *The Baltic Sea Regional Study on Adolescents' Sexuality*. Oslo: NOVA Norwegian Social Research (www.nova.no).

Gordon, L. (1989) *Heroes of Their Own Lives: The Politics and History of Family Violence*. London: Virago.

Gorin, S. (2004) *Understanding What Children Say: Children's Experiences of Domestic Violence, Parental Substance Misuse and Parental Mental Health Problems*. London: National Children's Bureau/Joseph Rowntree Foundation.

Gottfredson, M. and Hirschi, T. (1990) *A General Theory of Crime*. Stanford, CA: Stanford University Press.

Greer, C. (2007) 'New media victims and crime', in Davis, P., Francis, P. and Greer, C. (eds) *Victims, Crime and Society*. London: Sage.

Gregg, D. (2010) *FIPs: A Classic Case of Policy Based Evidence*. Centre for Crime and Justice (www. crimeandjustice.org.uk).

Gregory, J. and Lees, S. (1999) *Policing Sexual Assault*. London: Routledge

Guldberg, H. (2009) *Reclaiming Childhood: Freedom and Play in an Age of Fear*. London: Routledge.

Hackett, S. (2010) 'Harmful sexual behaviours', in Barter, C. and Berridge, D. (eds) *Children Behaving Badly: Peer Violence Between Children and Young People*. London: Wiley (pp. 121–136).

Hagemann-White, C. (2010) *European Commission Feasibility Study to Assess the Possibilities, Opportunities and Needs to Standardize National Legislation on Violence Against Women, Violence*

Against Children and Sexual Orientation Violence. Luxembourg: Publications Office of the European Union.

Haggerty, R., Sherrod, L., Garmezy, N. and Rutter, M. (eds) (1996) *Stress, Risk and Resilience in Children and Adolescents.* Cambridge: Cambridge University Press.

Hales, J., Nevill, C., Pudney, S. and Tipping, S. (2009) *Longitudinal Analysis of the Offending, Crime and Justice Survey 2003–06: Key Implications.* Research Report No. 19. London: Home Office.

Hall, S., Critcher, C., Jefferson, T., Clarke, J. and Roberts, B. (1980) *Policing the Crisis.* London: Macmillan.

Hanmer, J. and Griffiths, S. (2000) 'Policing repeated domestic violence by men: A new approach', in Hanmer, J. and Itzin, C. (eds) *Home Truths About Domestic Violence.* London: Routledge.

Hanmer, J. and Saunders, S. (1985) *Well Founded Fear.* London: Hutchinson.

Hansard (2011) Sir Michael Gove, 27 April (Column 211).

Heidensohn, F. (1985) *Women and Crime.* London: Macmillan.

HM Government (2003) *Every Child Matters.* London: Stationery Office.

HM Government (2007) *Children's Plan.* London: Department for Children, Schools and Families.

HM Government (2008a) *Staying Safe Action Plan.* London: Department for Children, Schools and Families.

HM Government (2008b) *Youth Crime Action Plan.* London: Stationery Office.

HM Government (2009) *Youth and Crime Commission Consultation.* London: Stationery Office.

HM Government (2010a) *Call to End Violence Against Women and Girls* (www.homeoffice.gov.uk).

HM Government (2010b) *Call to End Violence Against Women and Girls Action Plan* (www.homeoffice.gov.uk).

HM Government (2011a) *A Child Centred System: The Government's Response to the Munro Review of Child Protection: July.* London: HMSO.

HM Government (2011b) *A Plain English Guide to the Localism Bill: Update.* London: Department for Communities and Local Government (www.communities.gov.uk).

Hester, M., Pearson, C. and Harwin, N. (2007) *Making an Impact: Children and Domestic Violence. A Reader* (2nd edn). London: Jessica Kingsley.

Heywood, C. (2001) *A History of Childhood.* Oxford: Polity Press.

Hickey, L., Vizard, E. and McCrory, E, (2005) *Links Between Juvenile Sexually Abusive Behaviour and Emerging Severe Personality Disorder Traits in Childhood.* London: DoH/Home Office/NOMS/DSPD.

Hilton, Z. (2011) Head of Research CEOP, personal communication.

Hirschi, T. (1969) *Causes of Delinquency.* Berkeley: University of California Press.

Hoare, J., Parfrement-Hopkins, J., Britton, A., Hall, P., Scribbins, M. and Flatley, J. (2011) *Children's Experience and Attitudes Towards the Police, Personal Safety and Public Spaces: Findings from the 2009/10 British Crime Survey Interviews with Children Aged 10 to 15 Supplementary Volume 3 to Crime in England and Wales 2009/10.* London: Home Office.

Home Affairs Committee (2010) *The Government's approach to Crime Prevention.* London: Stationery Office.

Home Affairs Committee (2011) *The Government's Approach to Crime Prevention: Government*

Response to the Tenth Report from the Committee Session 2009–10 Third Special Report of Session 2010–11. London: Stationery Office.

Home Office (2008) *Cutting Crime*. London: Home Office (www.homeoffice.gov.uk).

Home Office (2009a) *Recorded Crime 1898 to 2002*. London: Home Office.

Home Office (2009b) *Anti Social Behaviour Order Statistics England and Wales 2009*. London: Home Office (www.homeoffice.gov.uk).

Home Office (2010) *Homicides, Firearm Offences and Intimate Violence 2008-9, Supplementary Volume 2 to Crime in England and Wales, 2008–9*. London: Home Office.

Hooper, C. (2010) 'Gender, maltreatment and young people's offending', in Featherstone, B., Hooper, C., Scourfield, J. and Taylor, J. (eds) *Gender and Child Welfare in Society*. Chichester: Wiley-Blackwell.

Hough, M. and Mayhew, P. (1983) *The British Crime Survey*. London: Home Office.

House of Commons (2009) *House of Commons Home Affairs Committee Knife Crime Seventh Report of Session 2008–09* (HC 112–1). London: Home Office (www.parliament.gov.uk).

Howe, D. (2005) *Child Abuse and Neglect: Attachment, Development and Intervention*. London: Palgrave Macmillan.

Hoyle, C. (1998) *Negotiating Domestic Violence: Police, Criminal Justice Systems and Victims*. Oxford: Claredon Press.

Humphreys, C. and Stanley, N. (eds) (2006) *Domestic Violence and Child Protection*. London: JKP.

International Federation of Journalists (IFJ) (2002) *Putting Children in the Right: Guidelines for Journalists and Media Professionals*. Brussels: IFJ.

James, A. and James, A. (2004) *Constructing Childhood*. London: Palgrave.

Jenks, C. (1996) *Childhood*. London: Routledge.

Kellett, M. (2005) *How to Develop Children as Researchers*. London: Paul Chapman.

Kelly, L. (1988) *Surviving Sexual Violence*. Cambridge: Polity Press.

Kelly, L. (1991) 'Unspeakable acts abuse by and between women.' *Trouble and Strife*, 21: 13–20.

Kendall-Tackett, K. (2008) 'Developmental impact', in Finkelhor, D. *Childhood Victimization*. Oxford: Oxford University Press (pp. 65–91).

Kimborough-Melton, R. and Campbell, R. (2008) 'Strong communities for children: A community wide approach to prevention of child abuse and neglect.' *Family and Community Health*, 31(2): 100–112.

Kinsey, R., Lea, J. and Young, J. (1986) *Losing the Fight Against Crime*. Oxford: Blackwell.

Kiselica, M. and Morill-Richards, M. (2007) 'Sibling maltreatment: The forgotten abuse.' *Journal of Counselling and Development*, 85: 148–160.

Kitzinger, J. (1997) 'Who are you kidding? Children, power and the struggle against sexual abuse', in James, A. and Prout, A. (eds) *Constructing and Re Constructing Childhood* (2nd edn). London: Routledge (pp. 165–189).

Klahr, A., Mcgue, M., Iacono, W. and Burt, S. (2011) 'The association between parent–child conflict and adolescent conduct problems over time: Results from a longitudinal adoption study.' *Journal of Abnormal Psychology*, 120 (1): 46–56.

Krug, E. G., Dahlberg, L. L., Mercy, J. A., Zwi, A. B. and Lozano, R. L. (eds) (2002) *World Report on Violence and Health*. Geneva: World Health Organization.

Kurtz, P., Gaudin, J., Wodarski, J. and Howing, P. (1993) 'Maltreatment and the school-aged child: school performance consequences'. *Child Abuse and Neglect*, 17: 581–589.

Lamb, M., Orbach, Y., Hershkowitz, I., Esplin, P. and Horowitz, I. (2007) 'Structured forensic interview protocols improve the quality and informativeness of investigative interviews with children.' *Child Abuse and Neglect*, 31(11–12): 1201–1231.

Laming, Lord (2003) *The Victoria Climbié Inquiry: Report of an Inquiry by Lord Laming* (Cm 5730). London: HMSO.

Laming, Lord (2009) *The Protection of Children in England: A Progress Report*. London:DfE (https://www.education.gov.uk/publications/eOrderingDownload/HC-330.pdf accessed June 2011).

Land, K. (2010) *Child and Youth Well-being Index 2010*. Durham, NC: Duke University Press.

Lapierre, S. (2010) 'More responsibilities, less control: Understanding the challenges and difficulties involved in mothering in the context of domestic violence.' *British Journal of Social Work*, 40: 1434–1451.

Layard, R. and Dunn, J. (2009) *A Good Childhood: Searching for Values in a Competitive Age*. London: Children's Society/Penguin.

Lazenbatt, A. (2010) *The Health and Mental Health Impact of Child Maltreatment, Research Briefing*. London: NSPCC (www.nspcc.org.uk/Inform).

Lewis, J. (1996) 'Gender and welfare in the late nineteenth and early twentieth centuries', in Digby, A. and Stewart, J. (eds) *Gender, Health and Welfare*. London: Routledge (p. 2).

Lombroso, C. (1876) *L'Uomo Deliquente* (first published 1876), 5th edn 1897. Torina: Bocca.

Macy, R. (2007). 'A coping theory framework to preventing sexual revictimization.' *Aggression and Violent Behaviour*, 12: 177–192.

MacKinnon, C. (1989) *Towards a Feminist Theory of the State*. Cambridge, MA: Harvard University Press.

Maguire, M., Morgan, R. and Reiner, R. (eds) (2007) *The Oxford Handbook of Criminology*. Oxford: Oxford University Press.

Main, M. and Solomon, J. (1986) 'Discovery of an insecure disorganized/disoriented attachment pattern', in Braxelton, T. and Yogman, Y. (eds) *Affective Development in Infancy*. Norwood, NJ: Ablex.

Makarios, M. (2007) 'Race, abuse, and female criminal violence.' *Feminist Criminology* 2 (2): 100–116.

McAra, L. and McVie, S. (2007) *The Edinburgh Study of Youth Criminal Justice Transitions*. Edinburgh: Edinburgh Study of Youth Transitions (www.law.ed.ac.uk).

McGee, C. (2000) *Childhood Experiences of Domestic Violence*. London: Jessica Kingsley.

McVeigh, C., Hughes, K., Bellis, M., Reed, E., Ashton, J. and Syed, Q. (2005) *Violent Britain: People, Prevention and Public Health*. Liverpool: Centre for Public Health, John Moores University.

Mednick, W., Gabrielli, W. F. Jnr and Hutchings, B. (1984) 'Genetic influences in criminal convictions: evidence from an adoption cohort.' *Science* 24: 891–894.

Melhuish, E. *et al*. (2008) *The Impact of Sure Start Local Programmes on Three Year Olds and Their Families*. The National Evaluation of Sure Start (NESS). London: HMSO.

Mesie, J., Gardner, R. and Radford, L. (2007) *Towards a Public Service Agreement on Safeguarding*. DfES report (www.dcsf.gov.uk/research).

Messerschmidt, J. (1993) *Masculinities and Crime*. Maryland: Rowman & Littlefield.

Messerschmidt, J. (1994) 'Schooling, masculinities and youth crime by white boys', in Newburn T. and Stanko, E. *Just Boys Doing Business? Men, Masculinities and Crime*. London: Routledge (pp. 81–99).

Metro London (2011) Teenager 'hunted to death by gang', 10 March.

Millard, B. and Flattley, J. (2010) *Experimental Statistics on the Victimization of Children Aged 10 to 15: Findings from the British Crime Survey for the Year Ending December 2009. England and Wales Statistical Bulletin*. London: Home Office.

Ministry of Justice (2010a) *Statistics on Women and the Criminal Justice System*. London: MOJ.

Ministry of Justice (2010b) *Reoffending of Juveniles: Results from the 2008 Cohort England and Wales*. Ministry of Justice Statistics bulletin. London: MOJ.

Ministry of Justice (2010c) *Breaking the Cycle*: *Effective Punishment, Rehabilitation and Sentencing of Offenders* (Cm 7972). London: MOJ.

Ministry of Justice/Youth Justice Board (2011) *Strategy for the Secure Estate for Children and Young People in England and Wales Plan for 2011–12 and 2014–15 Consultation Document* (www.justice. gov.uk).

Mirlees-Black, C. (1999) *Domestic Violence Findings from the British Crime Survey Self Completion Questionnaire*. London: Home Office.

Moffitt, T. (1993) 'Adolescent limited and life course persistent anti social behaviour a developmental taxonomy.' *Psychological Review*, 100: 674–701.

Moffitt, T. E., Caspi, A., Harrington, H. and Milne, B. (2002) 'Males on the life-course-persistent and adolescence-limited antisocial pathways: Follow-up at age 26 years.' *Development and Psychopathology*, 14(1): 179–207.

Morgan, R. and Newburn, T. (2007) 'Youth Justice', in Maguire, M., Morgan, R. and Reiner, R. (eds) *The Oxford Handbook of Criminology*. Oxford: Oxford University Press (pp. 1024–1060).

Morley, R. and Mullender, A. (1994) *Children Living With Domestic Violence*. London: Whiting and Birch.

Mucurty, R. and Curling, A. (2008) *Review of the Roots of Youth Violence. Volume 1 Findings, Analysis and Conclusions*. Ontario: Queens Printers.

Mudaly, C. and Goddard, C. (2006) *The Truth is Longer Than a Lie: Children's Experiences of Abuse and Professional Interventions*. London: JKP.

Mullender, A. (1996) *Re-Thinking Domestic Violence*. London: Routledge.

Mullender, A. and Morley, R. (eds) (1994) *Children Living with Domestic Violence: Putting Men's Abuse of Women on the Child Care Agenda*. London: Whiting and Birch.

Mullender, A., Hague, G., Inman, U., Kelly, L., Malos, E. and Regan, L. (2003) *Children's Perspectives on Domestic Violence*. London: Sage.

Muncie, J. (1998) ' "Give 'em what they deserve": the young offender and youth justice policy', in M. Langan ed. *Welfare, Needs, Rights and Risks*. London: Routledge.

Munro, E. (2007) *Child Protection*. London: Sage.

Munro, E. (2010*) Part One: A System's Analysis*. London: Department for Education (http://www. education.gov.uk/munroreview/ accessed June 2011).

Munro, E. (2011a) *The Munro Review of Child Protection Interim Report: The Child's Journey*. London: Department for Education (http://www.education.gov.uk/munroreview/ accessed June 2011).

Munro, E. (2011b) *The Munro Review of Child Protection Final Report: A Child Centered System.* London: Department for Education (http://www.education.gov.uk/munroreview/ accessed June 2011).

Natale, L. (2010). *FACTSHEET—Youth Crime in England and Wales.* London: CIVITAS Institute for the Study of Civil Society.

National Centre for Social Research (NATCEN) (2010) *ASB Family Intervention Projects: Monitoring and Evaluation.* London: DCSF *Research Report* (https://www.education.gov.uk/publications/eOrderingDownload/DCSF-RR215.pdf accessed June 2011).

Newburn, T. (2007) 'Youth crime and youth culture', in Maguire, M., Morgan, R. and Reiner, R. (eds) *The Oxford Handbook of Criminology.* Oxford: Oxford University Press (pp. 575–601).

Newman, T. (2004) *What Works in Building Resilience?* London: Barnardos.

Nichols, S. (2011) 'Media representations of youth violence', in Barter, C. and Berridge, D. *Children Behaving Badly: Peer Violence Between Children and Young People.* London: Wiley (pp. 167–180).

Nofziger, S. (2009) 'Deviant lifestyles and violent victimization at school.' *Journal of Inter-personal Violence,* 24 (9): 1494–1517.

NSPCC (2006) *A Pocket History of the NSPCC.* London: NSPCC.

NSPCC (2007) Miles TV advert (www.nspcc.org.uk)

Ofsted (2010) *Children on Rights and Responsibilities: A Report of Children's View by the Children's Rights Director for England* www.rights4me.org

Olds, D., Eckenrode, J., Henderson, C., Kitzman, H., Powers, J., Cole, R., Sidera, K., Morris, P., Pettit, L. and Luckey, D. (1997) 'Long term effect of home visitation on maternal life course and child abuse and neglect: Fifteen year follow up of a randomised trial.' *Journal of American Medical Association,* 278: 637–643.

Papadopolous, L. (2009) *The Sexualization of Young People Review.* London: Home Office.

Parton, N. (1985) *The Politics of Child Abuse.* Basingstoke: Macmillan.

Parton, N. ed. (1997) *Child Protection and Family Support.* London: Routledge.

Parton, N. (2006) *Safeguarding Childhood,* London: Palgrave.

Pearson, G. (1983) *Hooligan: A History of Respectable Fears.* London: Macmillan.

Pinheiro, P. (2006) *World Report on Violence against Children.* New York: United Nations.

Piquero, A., Daigle, L., Gobson, C., Leper Piquero, N. and Tibbett, S. (2007) 'Research note: Are life course persistent offenders at risk for adverse health outcomes?' *Journal of Research on Crime and Delinquency,* 44(2): 185–207.

Povey, D., Coleman, K., Kiazo, P. and Roe, S. (2009) *Homicides, Firearm Offences and Intimate Violence 2007–08,* supplementary Volume 2 to *Crime in England and Wales 2007–08.* London: Home Office.

Prior, V. and Glaser, D. (2006) *Understanding Attachment and Attachment Disorders: Theory Evidence and Practice.* London: JKP.

Radford, L. (2004) 'Programmed or licensed to kill? The new biology of femicide' in Rees, D. and Rose, S. (eds) *The New Brain Science: Perils and Prospects.* Cambridge: Cambridge University Press (pp. 131–148).

Radford, L. and Hester, M. (2006) *Mothering Through Domestic Violence.* London: JKP.

Radford, L., Aitken, R., Miller, P., Roberts, J., Ellis, J. and Firkic, A. (2011) *Meeting the Needs of Children Living With Domestic Violence in London.* London: NSPCC/Refuge.

Radford, L., Corral, S., Bradley, C., Fisher, H., Bassett, C., Howat, N. and Collishaw, S. (2011) *Child Abuse and Neglect in the UK Today*. London: NSPCC. Available online at www.nspcc.org.uk/childstudy.

Rebellon, C., Straus, M. and Medeiros (2008) 'Self-Control in global perspective: an empirical assessment of Gottfredson and Hirschi's general theory within and across 32 national settings.' *European Journal of Criminology*, 5(3): 331–362.

Reder, P. and Duncan, S. (1999) *Lost Innocents: A Follow-Up Study of Fatal Child Abuse*. London: Routledge.

Rees, G. (1993) *Hidden Truths: Young People's Experiences of Running Away*. London: The Children's Society.

Rees, G., Gorin, S., Jobe, A., Stein, M., Medford, R. and Goswani, H. (2010) *Safeguarding Young People: Responding to Young People 11 to 17 Who Are Maltreated*. London: Children's Society.

Reiner, R. (2007) 'Media made criminality: The representation of crime in the mass media', in Maguire, M., Morgan, R. and Reiner, R. (eds) *The Oxford Handbook of Criminology*. Oxford: Oxford University Press (pp. 302–337).

Rich, A. (1984) *Of Woman Born: Motherhood as Experience and Institution*. London: Virago.

Richie, B. (1996) *Compelled to Crime: The Gender Entrapment of Black Battered Women*. London: Routledge.

Roe, S. and Ashe J. (2008) *Young People and Crime: Findings from the 2006 Offending, Crime and Justice Survey*. London: Home Office.

Runyan, D. (2000) 'The ethical, legal, and methodological implications of directly asking children about abuse.' *Journal of Interpersonal Violence*, 15(7): 675–681.

Rutherford, A. (1992) *Growing Out of Crime* (2nd edn). London: Pelican.

Rutter, M. (1996) 'Transitions and turning points in developmental psychopathology.' *International Journal of Behavioral Development*, 19: 603–626.

Rutter, M. (1998) *Anti Social Behaviour by Young People*. Cambridge: Cambridge University Press.

Rutter, M. (2007) 'Resilience, competence and coping.' *Child Abuse and Neglect*, 31: 205–209.

Smart, C. (1995) *Law Crime and Sexuality*. London: Sage.

Solomon, E. and Garside, D. (2008) *Ten Years of Labour's Youth Justice Reforms: an Independent Audit*. London: Hadley Trust (www.crimeandjustice.org.uk/opus647/youthjusticeaudit.pdf).

Spatz-Widom, C. (2000) *Childhood Victimization: Early Adversity Later Psychopathology*. National Institute of Justice Journal (www.ncjrs.gov/pdffiles1/jr00024b.pdf).

Stanko, B. (1985) *Intimate Intrusions*. London: Routledge.

Stanko, E. (1990) *Everyday Violence*. London: Pandora.

Stanley, N., Miller, P., Richardson Foster, H. and Thomson, G. (2010) *Children and Families Experiencing Domestic Violence: Police and Social Services Responses*. London: NSPCC (www.nspcc.org.uk/Inform).

Statham, J. and Chase, E. (2010) *Child Well-being A Brief Overview*. Briefing Paper. Childhood Well-being Research Centre, University of London/University of Kent/University of Loughborough.

Statistics Commission (2005) *PSA Targets: The Devil in the Detail*. London: Statistics Commission.

Stein, M., Rhys, G., Hicks, L. and Gorin, S. (2009) *Neglected Adolescents Literature Review*. Research Brief DCS-RBX-09-04; London: DCS (www.education.gov.uk).

Straus, M. and Smith, C. (1990) 'Family patterns and child abuse', in Straus, M. and Gelles, R. (eds) *Physical Violence in American Families: Risk Factors and Adaptations to Violence in 8145 Families*. New Brunswick, NJ: Transaction Publishers) available to download from http://pubpages.unh.edu/~mas2/VB32.pdf).

Straus, M. Gelles, R. and Steinmetz, S. (1980) *Behind Closed Doors: Violence in the American Family*. New York: Anchor Press.

Tremblay, R. and Nagin, D. (2004) 'Physical aggression during early childhood: Trajectories and predictors.' *Pediatrics*, 114(1): 43–50.

Tunstill, J. and Allnock, D. (2007) *Understanding the Contributions of Sure Start Local Programmes to the Task of Safeguarding Children's Welfare*, Report 026.NESS/2007/FR026. Available online at http:www.education.gov.uk/G0076846/the-studies-in-the-safeguarding-research-initiative/sslp-safegurding study.

UNICEF (2003) *A League Table of Child Maltreatment Deaths in Rich Nations*. Innocenti Report Card, 5, September. Florence: Innocenti Research Centre (www.unicef-icdc.org).

UNICEF (2007) *Child Poverty in Perspective: An Overview of Child Well-being in Rich Countries*. Innocenti Research Centre Report Card, 7. Florence: IRC (www.unicef.org/irc).

Vold, G., Bernard, T., and Snipes, J. (2002) *Theoretical Criminology* (5th edn). Oxford: Oxford University Press.

Walby, S. and Allen, J. (2004) *Domestic Violence, Sexual Assault and Stalking: Findings from the British Crime Survey*. London: Home Office.

Weijters, G., Scheepers, P. and Gerris, J. (2009) 'City and/or neighbourhood determinants? Studying contextual effects on youth. *Delinquency European Journal of Criminology*, 6(5): 439–455.

Wilson, D., Sharp, C. and Patterson, A. (2006) *Young People and Crime: Findings from the 2005 Offending, Crime and Justice Survey*. London: Home Office (www.homeoffice.gov.uk).

Wilson, H. and Spatz-Widom, C. (2011) 'Pathways from childhood abuse and neglect to HIV-risk sexual behavior in middle adulthood, *Journal of Consulting and Clinical Psychology*. Advance online publication. doi: 10.1037/a0022915 Feb 28th

Wong, T., Slotboom, A. and Bijleveld, C. (2010) 'Risk factors for delinquency in adolescent and young adult females: A European review.' *European Journal of Criminology*, 7(4): 266–284.

Index